3-MINUTE DEVOTIONS
for Families

Janice Thompson

3-MINUTE DEVOTIONS for Families

Janice Thompson

BARBOUR BOOKS
An Imprint of Barbour Publishing, Inc.

INTRODUCTION

Most days we're seeking out a moment or two of inspiration and encouragement—to come together as a family and spend time with God.

Here is a collection of moments from the true source of all inspiration and encouragement—God's Word. Within these pages you'll be guided through just-right-size readings that you can experience in as few as three minutes:

Minute 1: Reflect on God's Word
Minute 2: Read real-life application and
            encouragement
Minute 3: Pray

These devotions aren't meant to be a replacement for digging deep into the scriptures or for personal, in-depth quiet time. Instead, consider them a perfect jump start to help you form a habit, as a family, of spending time with God every day.

Your word is a lamp to guide my
feet and a light for my path.
PSALM 119:105 NLT

For am I now seeking the approval of man,
or of God? Or am I trying to please man?
If I were still trying to please man,
I would not be a servant of Christ.
GALATIANS 1:10 ESV

It's not always easy to remember that our work is for God, not people. From the time we're young we set out to please others—teachers, parents, friends, and so on. Then as we get older, we continue on in our people-pleasing ways, seeking to make professors, bosses, future in-laws, and many others happy. Even in our golden years we find ourselves wanting to please our grown children. There's never a point when we're free from the temptation to make others happy. Only when we let go of the desire to please people and set our sights on pleasing only God will we feel true release and joy. Our work has to be for Him and Him alone.

Father, may we, as a family, seek to please You above all
others. From the youngest to the oldest in our circle,
may we lay down our desires to be people pleasers
and choose only to be God-pleasers. Amen.

*Accept one another, then, just as Christ
accepted you, in order to bring praise to God.*
ROMANS 15:7 NIV

To be accepted means we're recognized or acknowledged.
Let's face it, we all want to be recognized. Maybe you're
part of a group (perhaps even your family) and no
one seems to pay attention to you. Here's some good
news today: God knows you. He recognizes you. He
acknowledges you. He believes in you. More than
anything, He wants you to know that you're His kid—you
belong to Him. And that same feeling of "acceptance"?
He wants you to share it with others, in your family and
all around you. When you accept people, you're treating
them the way God wants you to.

*We're so happy to be accepted by You, Lord.
You recognize us! Show us how to accept others, Father,
even the people who are really different from us.
We don't want to judge anyone.
We want to learn to be accepting and kind,
as You are accepting and kind. Today, please show
us how to do that with everyone we meet. Amen.*

PRAYER

"If my people, who are called by my name, will humble themselves and pray and seek my face and turn from their wicked ways, then will I hear from heaven, and I will forgive their sin and will heal their land."

2 CHRONICLES 7:14 NIV

Prayer is an essential part of the believer's life. If we claim to love God but don't spend time talking with Him—and listening to His voice—then our relationship will be weak, at best. The Word of God gives special promises to those who pray. When we humble ourselves, when we cry out to the Lord, turning away from our sin, then God not only hears. . .He forgives *and* heals. What does He heal? Our hearts, our families, our communities. Talk about the power of prayer!

Lord, You've called us to pray. Today, as a family, we ask that You woo us back into Your chambers, so that we can change the world. . .on our knees. You've promised that our prayers will change things— our family, our community, our world. We don't have all the answers, but You do. Thank You, Father. Amen.

Do everything without grumbling or arguing, so that you may become blameless and pure, "children of God without fault in a warped and crooked generation." Then you will shine among them like stars in the sky as you hold firmly to the word of life. And then I will be able to boast on the day of Christ that I did not run or labor in vain.

PHILIPPIANS 2:14–16 NIV

Do everything without grumbling? In a family environment? Is this realistic? With so many personalities at work, can we really live a complaint-free life? We might not get it right every time, but if we strive to put the needs of others above our own wants and wishes, the opportunity for peaceful cohabitation is possible. God longs for us to live at peace with one another so that we can shine like stars. Today, choose to put bickering aside, not just for peace in your own hearts, but so that others will learn from your example.

Lord, our family longs to live at peace. Show us how to get along—to forgive, to stop pointing fingers, and to lay down the need to be right. May true resolution come as selfishness is laid aside, we pray. Amen.

*" 'Love the Lord your God with all your heart and with all
your soul and with all your mind and with all your strength.'
The second is this: 'Love your neighbor as yourself.'
There is no commandment greater than these."*
MARK 12:30–31 NIV

Most believers know that loving God is key to a
successful life. Loving others isn't always as easy. Why?
Because (unlike God) the people in our lives let us down.
They fail. That's why it's so important to read the rest of
the verse. When we add "as yourself" it all begins to make
sense. We forgive ourselves for our flaws, don't we? Why
are we so hesitant to extend the same grace to those we
love? Truly loving them means we quickly let go of the
things that bring division. When we do this, His love
flows through us.

*Lord, thank You for the reminder that loving others—
even those who are difficult to love—is an important thing
we can do in this life. Show us how to do this, we pray.
Give us the courage to embrace grace, even in
the most complicated situations. Amen.*

Stick with what you learned and believed,
sure of the integrity of your teachers.
2 TIMOTHY 3:15 MSG

- - - - - - - - - - - - - -

From early childhood we're faced with lessons. ABCs, 123s, reading, writing, arithmetic. . .we're inundated. At every turn there's more to learn, and the lessons don't end when we graduate high school or college. Until the day we leave this life, we remain on a learning curve. Why should we think it would be any different in our spiritual walk? No matter how many times we're given a life-lesson, we still stumble and fall, then rise to try again. No matter our age, the spiritual learning curve continues. That's why it's so important to grace one another, especially in a family environment. Mess-ups? Sure, they're going to happen. Praise the Lord for His forgiveness and grace.

Father, You're such a wonderful teacher.
The way You instruct us is gentle, kind, and diligent.
We're so grateful that You have forgiven us,
the many times we've stumbled and fallen.
Thanks for picking us up, Lord.
May we extend that same grace to others. Amen.

If your enemy is hungry, give him food to eat;
if he is thirsty, give him water to drink.

PROVERBS 25:21 NIV

Families know what it's like to gather around the table
for a yummy meal. Laughter, conversation about the day,
and tasty, filling foods for the belly all draw us together.
Yes, it's easy to feed those we love, those we trust. Why,
then, does the Bible instruct us to feed our enemies? How
can we possibly extend generosity, joy, and that feeling
of "fullness" to those we can't stand? Sounds impossible.
And yet, that's exactly what we're called by God to do.
Extend a hand of friendship to an enemy? Yes, for true
peace comes as we learn to live in peace with others. It's
not always easy, but it's definitely worth it.

Lord, we love the time we spend around the table
with our family. What a wonderful time to swap stories
and laugh. Feeding those we love is easy. Today we ask
that You show us how we can "feed" our enemies,
even when it seems impossible. Amen.

*But Jonah ran away from the LORD and headed for
Tarshish. He went down to Joppa, where he found a ship
bound for that port. After paying the fare, he went aboard
and sailed for Tarshish to flee from the LORD.*

JONAH 1:3 NIV

- -

Oh boy. We all know what that "I wish I could just run
away from this problem" feeling is like. Sometimes we
face things that are so difficult we just want to bolt out
of the door. Jonah surely knew this feeling, too. But God
calls us to be courageous, even in the face of tough things.
No, it's not easy. But if we run—and we often do—we
usually end up having a "belly of the whale" experience.
No fun! So, stick close to God and do as He commands,
even if it's really, really hard.

*Lord, sometimes we just want to run! The things
You ask us to do seem impossible. But You know best,
Father. We don't want to end up in the belly of a whale.
Show us, in each circumstance, how to walk in obedience,
so that we can be in the center of Your will. Amen.*

VALUABLE!

"Fear not, therefore; you are of more
value than many sparrows."
MATTHEW 10:31 ESV

- -

No matter our age, we still struggle with feelings of inadequacy. When we're young we compare ourselves to our classmates. When we're older, we compare houses, bank accounts, even the cars we drive. If we don't measure up—by the world's standards—we somehow feel less than. Isn't it wonderful to realize that God sees more value in us than many sparrows? And isn't it fascinating that we don't have to do anything to earn this value? It's not our works that earn us brownie points with our heavenly Father. . .He adores us and sees our value, simply because we're His.

Lord, we're so grateful for Your love. Thank You for
giving us value, simply because we're Your children.
When we're with You we have no feelings of
inadequacy, Father. Thank You for showing us
that we have value. Amen.

FACING BIG OBSTACLES

A champion named Goliath, who was
from Gath, came out of the Philistine camp.
His height was six cubits and a span.
1 SAMUEL 17:4 NIV

Obstacles. Ugh. How we dread them. They loom before us, seemingly huge and impenetrable. We face them with fear and trembling, wondering if we should crawl over them, trudge around them, or somehow try to tunnel through them. Rarely do we see them as what they are: temporary. May we begin to see life's hurdles through the filter of the Holy Spirit. They may look like the mighty Goliath, but even he fell to the ground when a young boy with God-sized faith looked him in the eye and tossed a few stones his way. Obstacles? They're no big deal when God's on your side.

Father, we're so glad that the obstacles in our
family's life aren't a big deal to You. Thank You for
reminding us that Goliath might've looked powerful,
but was weak in comparison to young David,
who was faith-filled. We want to be like David, Lord.
Give us God-sized faith, we pray. Amen.

STANDING FIRM

*Finally, my brethren, be strong in the Lord
and in the power of His might. Put on the
whole armor of God, that you may be able
to stand against the wiles of the devil.*
EPHESIANS 6:10–11 NKJV

Whenever we see something evil—or scary—coming our
way, we have a tendency to turn on our heels and run. Or
hide in a corner. Or pull the covers over our head. Rarely
do we see ourselves standing and facing the enemy as
he heads our way, but that's exactly what the Word of
God encourages us to do. Instead of fleeing, digging in
our heels and staring the enemy in the eye will be most
beneficial.

*Lord, thank You for giving us the courage to stand.
When we're dressed in Your holy armor, we're safe,
even when the enemy rises up against us. We will
always be victors with You on our side! Amen.*

*"I will set My rain-bow in the cloud,
and it will be something special to see because of
an agreement between Me and the earth."*
GENESIS 9:13 NLV

Most of us don't like to think about the possibility of a
burglar coming into our home and stealing our stuff. We
cringe, just pondering the what-ifs. Stealing "stuff" is
one thing; stealing our hope is another! So many times
we allow the enemy to rob us of this very valuable tool!
God never meant for us to be without hope. Why do
you think He placed the rainbow in the sky after Noah
landed on Mt. Ararat? Whenever Noah saw those brilliant
colors, so beautifully aligned, he remembered God's
promise. . .and it gave him hope. In the same way, we must
remember God's promises to us. When we do, we'll never
be hopeless. The next time the enemy tries to steal hope
from us, we have to realize he's up to tricks, and we can't
let him win.

*We don't have to wait for a rainbow
in the sky, Father. All we have to do is
remember Your promises—that You will be with us,
that You will never leave or forsake us. Amen.*

*Always be humble, gentle, and patient, accepting
each other in love. You are joined together
with peace through the Spirit, so make every
effort to continue together in this way.*
EPHESIANS 4:2–3 NCV

- -

Humble? Gentle? Patient? In a family environment? More
often than not, we're looking out for number one, which
means humility goes right out the window. Sometimes
we're not very gentle either—with our siblings, our
children, our parents. Let's face it. . .people are tough to
live with. That's why it's so good to read verses like this
one, because we need the reminder that God's kids (no
matter what age) are expected to treat others the same
way He treats us. How long do we have to keep this up?
Forever!

*Lord, we have to admit that we're not always as
gentle or patient as we should be. Sometimes we
want what we want and we want it right now.
It's so easy to forget that You've commanded us to treat others
as You would treat them. May we never forget, Father!
We want to love like You love. Amen.*

"Give, and it will be given to you. A good measure, pressed down, shaken together and running over, will be poured into your lap. For with the measure you use, it will be measured to you."

LUKE 6:38 NIV

- - - - - - - - - - - - - - - - - - - -

We don't give to get. (How selfish would that be?) And yet the Word of God is undeniable: If we give, it will be given back to us. And not just given back a little: Our generosity will be repaid above and beyond what we can imagine. What a remarkable way to live, as givers. As children, we can give. As teens, we can give even more. And as adults, there are countless ways we can bless others with our giving. It's time to get out of the box and think of giving as more than financial. We can give of our time, our talents, and our treasures. When people look at our family they can say, "Wow, now those are some generous people!"

Father, may our family be known for our giving—not just financial, but time, talents, and treasures. May we learn to be generous in all things, Lord. Amen.

NO CONDEMNATION

Therefore, there is now no condemnation
for those who are in Christ Jesus.
ROMANS 8:1 NIV

- -

What does it mean to condemn? To condemn someone means to put them down. To convict them. To rebuke or judge them. We're so quick to judge others, aren't we? Sometimes we're just as quick to judge ourselves. We don't forgive ourselves for our mistakes, our mess-ups. If you're struggling in this area, read today's scripture again. The Bible says there's to be no condemnation for those who are in Christ Jesus. If you have accepted Him as your Lord and Savior, He's wiped away all of your sins. You don't have to roll around in them anymore. You don't have to wonder where you stand with Him. The Lord sees you like a spotless lamb—white as snow. So, no judgment! Don't judge others. . .and don't judge yourself. There's only one Judge and He adores you, even when you mess up.

Lord, thank You for the reminder that we're not the judge and jury. We're Your kids (no matter our ages) and You forgive us when we make mistakes. We're so grateful for Your grace and mercy, Father. Amen.

THE RIGHT PATH

Direct your children onto the right path,
and when they are older, they will not leave it.
PROVERBS 22:6 NLT

Walking down a lovely path can be such a peaceful experience, especially when we know where it's leading us. The path guides us to where we need to go. We don't waver to the right or the left; we just stick to the road ahead of us, which is clearly mapped out. Living in a family environment is a bit like that, only we're not always sure where we're headed or what weeds we might encounter along the way. Sometimes the path isn't as clearly marked or has a lot of bumps. During those seasons we have to pray and trust God to guide us. He will! He's the best guide ever.

Thank You, Lord, for placing our feet on the right path.
May we never veer from it. We're trusting You to guide
us every step of the way, Father, even when the road gets
bumpy. What a wonderful guide You are, Lord. We're so
grateful for Your spiritual GPS. Amen.

OOO, BITTER!

*Let all bitterness and wrath and anger and clamor
and slander be put away from you, along with all malice.
Be kind to one another, tenderhearted, forgiving one
another, as God in Christ forgave you.*
EPHESIANS 4:31–32 ESV

- -

Have you ever taken a bite of a bitter lemon? It's hard to
swallow, isn't it? It leaves a sour taste in your mouth, too.
Even though we don't mean to, sometimes we grow bitter.
We let things fester to the point where the ongoing sour
taste remains, long after the incident. Think about how
you turn lemons into lemonade, by adding a bit of sugar.
Forgiveness is like sugar. It sweetens what was once bitter
and makes it tasty again. Today, if you're dealing with a
sour disposition or lingering unforgiveness, reach for the
sugar bowl. Just a spoonful will change your situation,
and possibly your relationships.

*Father, we have to admit, we've been guilty of holding
onto bitterness at times. It's easy to do. Today we ask
that You help us let go of the anger. We want to forgive.
Please help us do that, Lord, we pray. Amen.*

GENERATIONS

One generation shall praise Your works to another,
and shall declare Your mighty acts.
PSALM 145:4 NASB

- -

Generations. Have you ever pondered that word? Think of the generations of your family like stairsteps. Those who came before us laid a foundation. From there, the steps traveled up, up, up until they got to you! And the staircase will continue to get taller and taller long after you're gone. Your children (or those you mentor) will continue the work you started and they will, in turn, pass on the legacy to their children (or others they mentor). And so on and so on. When we give our lives to the Lord, when we commit to make a difference in the world, that legacy can be life-changing, not just for our families, but for all of the many people looking on.

Oh Father! What a wonderful thing, to watch our family
grow and change. When we think of our parents,
our grandparents, our great-grandparents, we can't help but
think of the legacy they left. How proud we are to pass that
legacy down to our children as well. Thank You, Lord. Amen.

CHOICES

*I want to do what is good, but I don't. I don't want to do
what is wrong, but I do it anyway. But if I do what I don't
want to do, I am not really the one doing wrong;
it is sin living in me that does it.*
ROMANS 7:19–20 NLT

- - - - - - - - - - - - - - - - - - -

Oh, how we want to do the right thing. Rarely do we set
off to do the wrong thing. Many times poor choices are
made on the fly, in the moment. We feel panicked and
make the wrong decision then we live to regret it. As long
as we're alive on planet earth it will be this way. It's part of
being human, of being imperfect. That said, we're created
in the image of a perfect God who longs for us to emulate
Him in every way. Even though we're bound to fail on
occasion, we need to try to do what is right. We can't let
sin have the upper hand. When we fall, we get back up
and try again. We don't give in to the temptation to stay
down for long. So, don't get off-course. Follow the example
of Jesus, who showed us how to live.

*Father, thank You for your grace, and thank You, too,
for teaching us that we can follow Your lead.
We don't have to let sin rule us. Amen.*

You changed my sorrow into dancing. You took away my clothes of sadness, and clothed me in happiness.
PSALM 30:11 NCV

- - - - - - - - - - - - - - - - - - - -

We all go through seasons of mourning. When we're in the middle of them, we can't see past the pain. We don't think about a happy tomorrow or a blissful season ahead. We only think about what we're going through at that very moment, and we're convinced the pain will last a lifetime. Even in a family environment, with different emotions at play, we're tempted to get down and stay down. That's why it's so important to remember that God moves in seasons. What you're going through right now—good or bad—won't last forever. There really will come a day when you look back and say, "Wow, I remember how tough that was." And you'll do it without the agonizing pain in your heart. God promises to turn our sorrow into dancing. No, it doesn't happen overnight. Yes, it does happen.

Father, we admit. . .our family has been through some stuff that seemed to drag on for a while. We wondered if we'd ever be okay again. We're so grateful for this reminder that pain doesn't last forever, Lord. Thank You so much for the reminder. Amen.

REJECTION

"If the world hates you,
you know it hated Me before it hated you."
JOHN 15:18 NLV

- - - - - - - - - - - - - - - - - - - -

We all want to be loved, accepted, part of the crowd. Being hated is no fun. No one wants to be rejected and despised. Those feelings can be brutal, but they don't have to last forever. If you're going through a season where you've been pushed out of your circle of friends, don't let it get you down, at least not for long. Don't place your value on what people think of you (or don't think of you). Remember, Jesus Himself was despised and rejected by men. And we have this assurance, that He understands. He's walked a mile in our shoes, in other words. It brings great comfort to know that He "gets" us (emotionally and otherwise) when we're hurting. What's the greatest lesson we can learn from Him as He heals our broken hearts? Not to reject others. Now there's a lovely lesson, indeed.

Lord, thank You for the assurance that You still love us,
even when others don't seem to. Amen.

NO DARKNESS

This is the message we heard from Jesus and now declare to you: God is light, and there is no darkness in him at all. So we are lying if we say we have fellowship with God but go on living in spiritual darkness; we are not practicing the truth.
1 JOHN 1:5–6 NLT

These are dark times. There's no denying it. Sometimes we worry for our families. We wonder if the innocence of youth is long gone, replaced with fear and other negative emotions that come from watching the nightly news. As parents, we wonder if our children can possibly escape the never-ending onslaught of advertising that threatens to steal their purity. That's when we have to remember that God is light. There's no darkness in Him. As long as we, as a family, remain in Him, we can overcome the evil in this world. If we choose darkness over light then we're not practicing truth. May our family be known as truth-tellers and truth-livers.

*Lord, may we always choose to live in Your light.
Keep us from all spiritual darkness.
Woo us with Your light. Amen.*

GODLY WISDOM

A wise man is strong, yes,
a man of knowledge increases strength.
PROVERBS 24:5 NKJV

- - - - - - - - - - - - - - - - - - - -

Isn't it funny how we look anywhere and everywhere for wisdom? A doctor gives a diagnosis and we go straight to the web to look it up. A friend is going through depression and we research "how to deal with someone in depression." How lovely would it be if our first stop on the research train was at the feet of the One who gives the best possible advice? Our wisdom, no matter what we're going through, should come first from God. He'll enlighten us, sure, and give us direction. But when we seek Him first, then we have clarity on where to go next. God's wisdom trumps human knowledge every time.

Lord, thank You for granting us wisdom—not head
knowledge, but a true, lasting wisdom from on high.
We're so grateful that Your wisdom (not our education)
increases our strength, Father. Amen.

GIVE IT YOUR ALL

Concentrate on doing your best for God, work you won't be ashamed of, laying out the truth plain and simple.
2 TIMOTHY 2:15 MSG

- -

Doing our best. As children, the point is driven home to us: Do your best on that test! Do your best on that ball team! Do your best memorizing verses for Sunday school! As adults we're still inundated with the "best" message: Give it your all at work! Be the best possible housekeeper, mom, dad, worker, friend, etc. you can be. It's not a bad message. Not at all. But we have to remember that even our very best is nothing until the Spirit of God breathes life into it. Today, instead of just striving, striving, striving, why not concentrate on asking God to be at the center of all you do, so that your work will be supernaturally empowered from on high.

Father, thank You so much for stirring up a "best is best" mentality so that we can give You our all.
We're grateful for Your patience with us, Lord. Amen.

Therefore, as God's chosen people, holy and dearly loved,
clothe yourselves with compassion, kindness,
humility, gentleness and patience.
COLOSSIANS 3:12 NIV

- -

People give so much thought to what they wear. They spend hours shopping for just the right clothes, shoes, and accessories. They lay out their clothes a day ahead of time, making sure they have all of the right pieces for the ensemble. Isn't it interesting how much time and effort we put into our clothing when we often put so little time into dressing ourselves in compassion, kindness, humility, gentleness, and patience, like today's verse says? What if we planned for those things in advance? What if, every night when we put our head on the pillow, we thought about how we would clothe ourselves the following day with all of these things? Let's make a spiritual fashion statement. Tomorrow, before slipping on your shoes, shirt, or slacks, put on love. The world will sit up and take notice.

Lord, we want to make a spiritual fashion statement.
Please don't let us forget that the most important part
of our wardrobes is love. Amen.

*This is the confidence we have in approaching God:
that if we ask anything according to his will, he hears us.
And if we know that he hears us—whatever we ask—
we know that we have what we asked of him.*
1 JOHN 5:14–15 NIV

Confidence. We work so hard to get it and do our best to instill it in our family. But where does confidence come from? Think about the story of Adam and Eve. After disobeying God, they were ashamed. They wouldn't look Him in the eye. It's the same with us. Our confidence is often shaken because we see ourselves as flawed. Messed up. Sinners. People who can't seem to get it right. Oh, but God sees us differently! No matter our age, He sees us as forgiven. Grace-filled. Born again. That should renew our confidence in a hurry. And when we have this kind of confidence, we know we can approach His throne with every request and He will hear us. What a wonderful God we serve!

*Father, thank You for the reminder that we can ask
according to Your will and You will hear us,
no matter what. Amen.*

God never changes his mind about the people
he calls and the things he gives them.
ROMANS 11:29 NCV

Have you ever decided to do something and then changed your mind afterward? Maybe you gave some thought to a certain job—or a certain class in school—then backed out. You shifted gears. Went a different direction. Or maybe someone you trusted promised you something, said they would do it, and then didn't. They had a change of heart. Humans are always changing their minds, aren't they? Isn't it comforting to know that God never changes His mind? If He said it, He will do it! When He calls us, it's forever. He won't send an e-mail saying, "You know, I've been thinking about this, and I'd like to rescind that call on your life." No way! If He said it, you can take it to the bank!

Father, have we paused to thank You lately for the call
You've placed on our lives? Thank You for calling everyone
in our family. We make a great team, as long as we put You
at the helm. Grateful, grateful! Amen.

THE NARROW ROAD

*"Strive to enter through the narrow door. For many,
I tell you, will seek to enter and will not be able."*
LUKE 13:24 ESV

- -

Remember, back in the olden days, when we used maps?
Every time Mom, Dad, Grandma, or Grandpa set off on
a road trip, out would come that huge paper map, with
the folds perfectly creased. If we really took our traveling
seriously, we invested in a road atlas. These days, we have
access to nearly every road with the push of a button.
Our GPS guides us every step of the way. We can decide
whether to take a super-highway or a quiet back road.
The point is, we have choices. Life is like that, too. There
are so many choices! So many roads we could be taking.
The Holy Spirit—our internal compass—is much like
a spiritual GPS. If we're listening, really listening, He
will guide us to that narrow path, the one that takes us
straight to our Father's arms.

*Father, it's easier to take a wide road. But You've called us
to walk a narrow road, one where You're in charge.
Today we choose to stay on the narrow road, Lord.
Help us, every step of the way, we pray. Amen.*

Greater love hath no man than this,
that a man lay down his life for his friends.
JOHN 15:13 KJV

- -

We live in a "me, myself, and I" generation, don't we? Everyone is looking out for number one. The problem with this approach is that it flies in the face of what the Bible teaches. God wants us to be others-focused, to the point where we would be willing to lay our very lives down for those we love. Today, pause and ask the Lord how you can shift your focus from self to others. Then, specifically ask Him how you can go out of your way to bless someone in particular—going above and beyond. What fun it is, to put others first!

Lord, it's not easy to lay down your life for others.
This we're learning first-hand. We tend toward selfishness.
Please remove all self-centeredness from our hearts today,
we pray. May we be a reflection of You in all we do,
always looking out for the needs of others. Amen.

GRATITUDE

A God-like life gives us much when we are happy
for what we have. We came into this world with nothing.
For sure, when we die, we will take nothing with us.
If we have food and clothing, let us be happy.
1 TIMOTHY 6:6–8 NLV

- - - - - - - - - - - - - -

Have you ever paused to think about how you came into
the world? We arrived on this planet, wailing babies—
completely naked and anxious for our first meal. Just as
we arrived with nothing clenched in our fists, we will exit
this life the very same way. All of the material possessions
we acquire—homes, cars, boats, clothes, jewels—will stay
behind and eventually lose their value. Perhaps this
is why the Lord is so intent on us having an attitude
of gratitude for the things He gives us, large or small,
because He knows their true place in our lives. Today, let's
make a commitment to express our gratefulness for all
that the Lord has provided. Do you have food? Clothing?
Then praise Him!

Lord, we admit, we sometimes forget to praise You for the
things we already have—our clothing, our daily bread,
the place we live. We choose to praise You today, Father,
for all of those things. We're truly grateful. Amen.

STARTING OVER

Therefore, if anyone is in Christ, he is a new creation.
The old has passed away; behold, the new has come.
2 CORINTHIANS 5:17 ESV

Starting over. Contemplate those two words, if you will.
How many times do we "start over" in this life? We start a
diet, then fall off the wagon, then start again. We make up
our minds to live on a budget, then make poor decisions,
then begin again. We promise ourselves we'll spend more
time with the Lord, then get distracted, then begin again.
Aren't you glad God is in the "starting over" business?
He doesn't look at our failures. He's not interested in
focusing on the wagon we've fallen off of. He's only
interested in picking us up, dusting us off, and putting
us back on the road to success once more. What wagon
have you fallen off of recently? Don't worry about it! Just
make up your mind to try once more. God will honor your
faithfulness.

Lord, we're so grateful for second chances. And third
chances. And fourth. You are such an encouraging Father.
Thank You for giving us the tenacity to try again. Amen.

Be completely humble and gentle; be patient,
bearing with one another in love.
EPHESIANS 4:2 NIV

- -

Bearing with others. It's not always as easy as it sounds, even in a family environment. Sometimes it's easier to "bear with" those we don't have to actually live with. Sharing a home, living in close confines, makes "bearing" really tough at times. Those little things, the everyday annoyances, can grate on us. The next time you're tempted to stop "bearing," think of a mama bear. Her naughty little cub does a lot of things wrong. He's always getting into trouble. But she's still right there, nuzzled up next to him, poking him with her nose and guiding him every step of the way. "Bearing" is less about putting up with and more about loving, caring, guiding. So, "bear" away, no matter who or what you're dealing with. After all, God "bears" a lot with His kids, too.

Father, we admit that we don't always have a lot
of patience. Sometimes people get on our nerves.
The little things they do grate on us. Thank You for this
reminder that we need to be more like that mama bear,
sticking close and guiding, even when it's tough. Amen.

FETCH THE PRIZE!

I press toward the goal for the prize
of the upward call of God in Christ Jesus.
PHILIPPIANS 3:14 NKJV

- -

It seems we're always pressing toward something in
this life. No matter where we are, we want to be at the
next level. We want to get through school. Then college.
Then get a great job. Then we press toward a promotion.
A family. Getting our kids in college. Press, press, press.
It can get exhausting if we're not pressing toward the
things that God has called us to. That's why the most
important thing we should "press toward" is the goal for
the prize of the upward call of God in Christ Jesus. If we
put His desires above our own, if we respond to His call
instead of seeking our own path, then everything else
will fall into place.

Father, we're pressing. . .and pressing. . .and pressing some
more! We don't always feel like we're making progress
but we won't give up. Thanks for cheering us on,
every step of the way. We're so grateful. Amen.

So God created mankind in his own image,
in the image of God he created them;
male and female he created them.
GENESIS 1:27 NIV

All created in His image. Yet, all of us are unique.
Different from one another. How is that possible? Our
perfect Father has designed each of us with different
characteristics, different qualities, different personalities.
Perhaps God went to such trouble to make us all unique
so that we could minister to different types of people.
Not everyone will listen to the man in the suit. Some
want to hear the message from a kid on a surfboard. Or a
woman standing in line at the grocery store with a toddler
crying in the front of the cart. Point is, we're different for
a reason, but we're all exquisitely designed, created in the
image of a very, very creative God. And He never makes
mistakes!

When we look at all of the different members of our family,
we're amazed by Your great workmanship, Lord.
It's so fascinating to realize that we're all created
in Your image, and yet we're all completely different.
We love Your creativity, Father. Amen.

*"You are the light of the world. A town built
on a hill cannot be hidden."*
MATTHEW 5:14 NIV

- - - - - - - - - - - - - - - - - - -

Remember as a child, how you sang "Twinkle, Twinkle,
Little Star"? Oh, how marvelous, to think of the night
sky, filled with shimmering stars. Why are we so drawn
to stars as children? Because they sparkle against the
darkness. They offer light and hope. In much the same
way, we're called to be lights in this dark world. God
wants us to twinkle, twinkle—to let our lights shine,
so that people will see us and have hope when they're
walking through dark places in their lives. Think about
it for a moment. If all of the stars stopped twinkling, the
nighttime would be very dark. If all of us who love the
Lord stopped shining our lights, this dark world would be
a devastating place to live. We must shine on, even when
it's tough. People need light so that they can find their
way. We are that light, and we must keep shining.

*Lord, we must admit, we don't always feel like shining our
lights. Sometimes we just want to hide away and
pull the covers over our heads. Thank You for the reminder
that people are watching and they need the light. Amen.*

HEAD, SHOULDERS, KNEES, AND TOES

Even so the body is not made up of one part but of many.
1 CORINTHIANS 12:14 NIV

- -

What a creative God we serve! He designed the human body with so many different parts—all different, and yet all designed to work together for the common good. Hands have a different role than eyes. The nose has a different role than the elbow. But take away any one of them and what a challenge we would face! It's the same in the body of Christ. We're all so different, with a variety of gifts and opinions. But God has knit us together as brothers and sisters, all part of one large body of Christ. Take away any one and where would we be? At a loss! The next time your differences arise in the family, just remember God's creative design of the human body. That will put things in perspective!

God, You are so creative. What a fascinating Creator and Father You are! You made each of us unique from our brothers and sisters and yet part of the family. We can't do without one another. Thank You for that reminder. Amen.

*For everyone has sinned; we all fall short of God's glorious
standard. Yet God freely and graciously declares that we
are righteous. He did this through Christ Jesus when he
freed us from the penalty for our sins.*
ROMANS 3:23–24 NLT

Everyone: Every. One. That's how many people mess up.
Older people. Young people. People who seem to have
their act together. People who can't seem to get anything
right. People in America. People in other countries.
All people sin. Everyone falls short of God's glorious
standard. Whew! Doesn't it make you feel better to know
you're not alone? But here's the really good part: Jesus
Christ, God's Son, paid the price for everyone. Every. One.
Everyone, everywhere. Every age. No matter who you are,
where you live, or what you've done, if you ask Jesus to be
your Lord and Savior, He will come into your heart and
offer forgiveness and new life.

*We make so many mistakes and sometimes we feel like
we're the only ones who just can't seem to get our acts
together. We feel relieved to know we're not the only ones
who get it wrong. Thank You for Your Son, who died for
everyone. Every. Single. One. Amen.*

FRIENDSHIP

After David had finished talking with Saul, Jonathan became one in spirit with David, and he loved him as himself. From that day Saul kept David with him and did not let him return home to his family. And Jonathan made a covenant with David because he loved him as himself.
1 SAMUEL 18:1-3 NIV

- - - - - - - - - - - - - - - - -

Oh, how we love our friends. They love us, too, even when we make mistakes. They encourage us, and tell us we can be successful. They even correct us when we're wrong, (in a loving way of course). When we find a true friend, he will stick with us, even when others don't. That's how it was with David and Jonathan. They were BFFs (best friends forever). They had an unspoken commitment, a bond they hoped would never be broken. BFFs love one another with a God-inspired love. They're pretty much inseparable. Everyone needs friends like that, don't they?

Lord, thank You so much for our friends.
They inspire us! What a blessing they are in our lives.
We're so grateful for each and every one. Amen.

"Who provides food for the raven when its young cry out to God and wander about for lack of food?"
JOB 38:41 NIV

- -

Have you ever been afraid that God wouldn't provide for your family? Maybe you had a pile of bills you couldn't pay or no money for groceries. Maybe your car was broken down or you lost your job and wondered if God would come through for you. What good news we find in today's verse! If the Lord cares about the birds of the air (the ravens) then how much more does He care about you? He provides for all of nature, and He will provide for you, His child, as well. Don't ever wonder if God will come through for you. Simply trust and then wait in expectation to see *how* He will come through.

Father, sometimes we find ourselves watching to see how You'll come through for our family. We go through lean seasons and we doubt. Thank You for this reminder that You care for the birds of the air. How much more You must care for our family, Lord! We're so grateful. Show us how to trust You more, Father. Amen.

SATISFIED

"I will abundantly bless her provision:
I will satisfy her needy with bread."
PSALM 132:15 NASB

We live in a day and age where people want, want, want.
New cars, new houses, new clothes, new electronics.
Newer, bigger, better. . .we want it all, and television
commercials convince us we deserve it all. How much
better would it be if we were satisfied with the things we
already had? God's heart is pleased when we show an
attitude of gratitude for the things He's already provided.
He's not opposed to "newer, bigger, better," but if our
focus is on those things and not on Him, then perhaps
they've become idols in our lives. And here's the really
cool thing: When we learn to be content, then God pours
out provision and abundance on us. Wow. Fascinating,
right? Satisfaction. Now, *that's* something to pray for.

Lord, we want to be satisfied in You! We don't want to
acquire "stuff" just because everyone around us has more,
more, more. Show us how to be content with what
You've already given. Teach us how to be satisfied
in Your presence, Lord. Amen.

A HAPPY VISION

Remember that story about Hansel and Gretel? They dropped bread crumbs as they walked through the forest so that they could find their way back. Then birds came along and ate the crumbs. Perhaps you can relate. You set out on life's journey, sure of where you're going, but then—before long—you can't seem to find the right path anymore. Perhaps it's time for a vision check. If God stirred your heart to move in a particular direction, then go back to Him and ask for a re-ignited vision. He will stir you to action again and give you a clear road to follow. Just stay focused, and He will guide you to where you need to go.

Lord, today we choose to re-focus on You: Your Word, Your personal messages to us, Your love. We want to move forward in the direction that You would have us, so help us keep our focus on You, Father. The road will be easier when we have clear direction. We're grateful for Your guidance. Amen.

*But the angel said to him, "Do not be afraid, Zacharias,
for your prayer is heard; and your wife Elizabeth will bear you
a son, and you shall call his name John."*
LUKE 1:13 NKJV

Did you know that God has answers to every question
even before we voice them? It's true! Many times we think
He's not paying attention or that He's not interested in
what we're going through, but nothing could be further
from the truth. He's interested, and He's already making
provision for our needs. So, next time you're tempted
to think, "Why bother praying? Does God even care?"
remember this verse. God knew Zacharias' prayer in
advance and already had an answer, long before the
questions were posed. He's longing to start giving you
creative answers, too. So why wait? Ask today, then watch
and see how our creative God responds!

*Father, we're so grateful that You hear us when we pray.
We're also grateful that You've already got an answer to
our questions before we ask them. We can trust You, Lord.
You've got this. What a relief! Amen.*

Strengthened with all might, according to his glorious power, unto all patience and longsuffering with joyfulness.
COLOSSIANS 1:11 KJV

The words *patience* and *longsuffering* often go together, don't they? Perhaps that's why we don't like to be patient, because we think there's going to be l-o-n-g suffering involved. The truth is, God doesn't teach us patience so that we'll suffer. He teaches us patience so that we appreciate His blessings when they come. The longer we wait for something good (think Christmas morning) the more excited we are about it when it arrives. So, instead of looking at patience as a bad thing, think of it in reverse. God is preparing us for something awesome! Wow! And when it comes, what a blessing it will be.

Lord, thank You for this reminder that patience has a payoff. You're not trying to withhold blessings; You're giving us an opportunity to appreciate them more when they arrive. We can't wait to see what You've got in store, Father. It's going to be great, and we're so excited. We praise You in advance, Lord. Amen!

"In the same way, let your light shine before others,
that they may see your good deeds and glorify
your Father in heaven."
MATTHEW 5:16 NIV

Are Christians expected to be "good deed doers?" Of course! Our good deeds don't earn us Brownie points with the Lord, but He's created us in His image, and He's the ultimate Good Deed Doer! We want to follow His example, which means that our deeds—our actions—must be good. When we live this way, we're shining His light and others are drawn to Him. Today, why not challenge yourself to be a "good deed doer," not to prove anything to God or others, but simply because it makes His heart happy? Ultimately, it will make your heart happy, too!

Lord, we don't mind admitting we've struggled a little with this whole "good works" thing. We know we're not saved by our good works (thank goodness), but we're saved to do good works. We're grateful for that reminder today, Father. Help us to shine our lights for You, not to earn points, but simply because it makes Your heart glad. Amen.

GRIEF

Be merciful to me, Lᴏʀᴅ, for I am in distress; my eyes grow weak with sorrow, my soul and body with grief.
PSALM 31:9 NIV

Many people look at grief as a bad thing, but it's really not. God gave us the emotions we have so that we'd have an outlet—a way to get things out in the open. When we're grieving, we're openly expressing (on the outside) what we're feeling on the inside. While it's not healthy to grieve for extended periods of time, it's equally unhealthy to turn your back on grieving. If you're going through a hard season, don't be afraid to let your emotions out. Your body and your heart will thank you.

*Father, thank You for the reminder that it's okay to grieve.
You gave us these emotions and we're so grateful.
Please help us to grieve on Your timetable.
May seasons of grief be short-lived. Amen.*

GENEROSITY

*"In all things I have shown you that by working hard
in this way we must help the weak and remember
the words of the Lord Jesus, how he himself said,
'It is more blessed to give than to receive.' "*

ACTS 20:35 ESV

- -

God loves a cheerful giver. We've heard this all of our
lives. We've also heard things like, "It's better to give than
to receive," which is also true. Why does God care so
much about generosity? Because He's a generous God,
and we're created in His image to be generous! Think
about His generosity for a moment: He's lavished us with
spiritual gifts, with new life in Christ, with thousands of
biblical promises. He's given us all that we need to thrive
in this lifetime. What a wonderful example He has set.
May we all learn by example that generosity is truly a
godly gift.

*Father, thank You for being so generous with us.
We're so grateful for all You've given. Now teach us how
to be generous, Lord. We want to be known as people
who give, not just people who receive. May we be
a reflection of You. Amen.*

Is anyone among you in trouble? Let them pray.
Is anyone happy? Let them sing songs of praise.
JAMES 5:13 NIV

Have you ever gone to the doctor with a sore throat or earache? Maybe you left his office with a prescription in hand, one guaranteed to put an end to your troubles, at least temporarily. A doctor's prescription is specifically designed to meet your need at that moment. God is the Great Physician. He cares about your health, sure, but He's also concerned about your thoughts, your heart, and your relationships. He's got prescriptions that work, no matter what ails you. What are these prescriptions? Prayer and praise. Those two prescriptions are absolutely guaranteed to cure you of whatever has you down, and they're absolutely free. You don't even have to go to a doctor to get them. And they're fast-acting, too! Just a few verses of a praise chorus and you'll be back on your feet in no time.

Father, we're so grateful You know what we need even
before we need it. Thank You for giving us this
prescription for happiness. So grateful! Amen.

DISCIPLINE

Because the L ORD disciplines those he loves,
as a father the son he delights in.
P ROVERBS 3:12 NIV

Discipline. We read the word and sigh. As children,
we're often disciplined. Why? To narrow the broad path
and give us direction. If we're not disciplined we have
too many choices, too many options, and most of them
don't end well. As we age, the types of discipline shift
and change, but we still go through it. Discipline by
professors. Discipline at work. Even discipline from the
Lord, as He gently loves and corrects. Instead of dreading
discipline, we should look forward to it. After all, the Lord
only disciplines those He loves. If you're going through
an "Oops!" period and sense the Lord's nudging to do
things differently next time, just remember that He's only
showing you a better way because He loves you so much.
Knowing that changes everything.

Lord, we'll take the discipline and thank You for it,
because we know it's for our own good. We'll keep growing
and changing as You shape us into Your image.
Bless You for Your patience. Amen.

"For I know the plans I have for you, declares the LORD,
plans for welfare and not for evil,
to give you a future and a hope."
JEREMIAH 29:11 ESV

Oh, how we love to make plans. We strategize, organize, and take off running, before we even pause to ask the Lord's opinion. How much better would it be to stop and pray and then ask what His plans are. The things that God has in store for us are wonderful, after all. They're far greater than anything we could dream up for ourselves. So, today, before putting one foot in front of the other, take a moment to ask the Lord, "What are Your plans, Father?" He will surely guide you into all that He has for you, and the outcome will be greater than you could've ever imagined.

Lord, thank You for the reminder that our plans, while
good, aren't always the best. You've got things in mind
for us that we can't even see. . .roads that we haven't even
walked yet. That brings us such peace! Amen.

55

I have told you this, so that you might have peace in your hearts because of me. While you are in the world, you will have to suffer. But cheer up! I have defeated the world.
JOHN 16:33 CEV

Remember when you were a little kid, having a bad day? Your mom or dad would say, "Cheer up!" It's hard to "cheer up" when you're feeling blue, isn't it? People can plaster smiles on their faces and encourage you to pretend everything is great when it's not, but unless you really believe it, what's the point? Here's the point! God reminds us in His Word that suffering will come, but He has overcome the world! He's defeated it, in fact. When we come to grips with this, we can lift our eyes and our hearts, even in the midst of the battle, because we know that we are already victorious in Him. Now, there's a reason to praise!

Thank You for caring enough about our family to remind us that You have defeated the world. With this reminder, we really can cheer up. Amen.

A FRUITY FAMILY

"Make a tree good and its fruit will be good,
or make a tree bad and its fruit will be bad,
for a tree is recognized by its fruit."
MATTHEW 12:33 NIV

- - - - - - - - - - - - - - - - - - - -

A family is made up of individuals, each unique from the other. Every person in the family is a different version of "fruity." When you bring them all together into one unit, you've got amazing variety—a fruit salad, if you will. Some are sweet. Some are a little more sour. But think once again about that fruit salad. When you mix it all together, the whole thing tastes great. The sweet and sour blend together into one delicious dish. We are all are created in the image of God. He intends for all of our quirks, all of our unique attributes, to merge into one delightful, useable unit, so that our family is known to others as "good fruit." Maybe it's time for a fruit inspection today. Toss out the bad fruit (the attributes, not the people), and work on making things yummy so that others will be drawn to your family and ultimately drawn to the Lord.

May we be known for our good fruit, Father. Love.
Joy. Peace. Longsuffering. Yes, all of these
things and more. Amen.

NOW I LAY ME DOWN TO SLEEP

I lie down and sleep; I wake again,
because the LORD sustains me.
PSALM 3:5 NIV

- - - - - - - - - - - - - - - - - - -

Ah, sleep! How we love it. There's nothing more satisfying after a long day's work than tumbling into bed, pulling the covers up, and nodding off. Sweet dreams, pleasant hours to rest our minds and hearts from the stresses of life. God longs for our family to be well rested so that we can accomplish more during our "awake" hours. When we're exhausted, we're unable to function at our best. So, hard as it might be with our busy schedules, we've got to pay attention to the hours we spend snoozing. This isn't wasted time. On the contrary, God built our bodies to require sleep. (Did you ever think about that? He could've designed us to stay awake 24-7, but He opted for a human body that requires rest.) God rested, too, you know. The Sabbath (seventh-day rest) was ordained so that we could get refreshed and reignited for the work ahead.

Father, we need our rest so that we can be more effective for You during the daylight hours. May You grant us sweet, peaceful sleep so that we wake up refreshed. Amen.

May the favor of the Lord our God rest on us;
establish the work of our hands for us—yes,
establish the work of our hands.
PSALM 90:17 NIV

Teamwork. How we need it in life. Every person on the team has a different role to play, but each role is critical to the survival of the team. This is especially true in the family environment. We all want to live as one big happy family, but if we forget to work as a team, we get into trouble, especially if there are big tasks to be accomplished. When we all work together, even the biggest jobs get done. And best of all, God's favor rests on us. He establishes the work of our hands. And with the Lord on our team, we are invincible! We can conquer any foe and overcome any obstacle.

Lord, we're so grateful You've placed us on a team.
We're each part of a larger group—our family and our
spiritual family. Whew! What a relief to know we don't
have to accomplish everything on our own! Many hands
make light work. . .and we're so grateful. Amen.

A RENEWED MIND

*Do not be conformed to this world, but be transformed
by the renewal of your mind, that by testing you may
discern what is the will of God, what is good
and acceptable and perfect.*
ROMANS 12:2 ESV

Whenever we see the prefix *re-* in front of a word, it
always means "again." The Bible says that we can have a
renewed mind. That means our mind can become new
again. No matter how troubling our thought life has been
in the past, we can have positive, pure thoughts today
and tomorrow. And having a renewed mind isn't just
for adults. Children who've struggled with insecurities,
anger or feelings of not being valued can have their
thoughts renewed, too. The Lord longs to take all of those
old thoughts and replace them with new, godly ones. He
can restore, renew, and reinvigorate our minds, so let's
give Him the opportunity to do so by surrendering our
thoughts to Him today.

*As a family, we bow the knee to You, Father, and ask You
to shape us into Your image. We give ourselves to You,
servants for the Gospel. Amen.*

I know the LORD is always with me. I will not be shaken,
for he is right beside me.
PSALM 16:8 NLT

- -

Perhaps you remember that old song, "Me and My
Shadow." The interesting thing about our shadow is that
it never leaves us. We can't shake it! We can't always see
it, but with just the right amount of sunlight, it will make
a sudden appearance. We could think of God in much the
same way. Even though we can't see Him with our eyes,
He's right there besides us. Always. When we're walking
through frightening times we don't have to be afraid
because He's with us. When our family goes through a
rough patch, He's right there, guiding and leading. And
sometimes, just like that shadow, God's presence is so real
we can sense it. What a wonderful gift, to walk so closely
with our Lord!

Lord, how grateful we are that You are right beside us.
No matter what our family goes through—good, bad,
or otherwise—we don't ever have to wonder if You're aware or
if You care. You're right there, just a prayer away, and Your
love is evident. Thank You, Father, for sticking close. Amen.

Do nothing out of selfish ambition or vain conceit.
Rather, in humility value others above yourselves.
PHILIPPIANS 2:3 NIV

Pride is a strange beast. It rears its head when you least expect it, and sometimes in ways you don't expect. It can show up as arrogance, but sometimes it masquerades as insecurity. Anything that points attention to self, after all, is pride. God calls us to lay aside our selves, lay down our pride, and focus solely on Him. It's one thing to say we put others ahead of ourselves, but another thing altogether to actually do it. We can't operate out of selfish ambition. Think about that for a moment. So much of what we do is really motivated by our own ambition, after all. But God always calls us to love others first, to value them and to focus on the greater good, not just what's good for us. Not easy, but definitely God's plan for a humble lifestyle.

Lord, we've learned so much about humility by getting to know Your Son. Jesus humbled Himself, becoming our sacrifice on the cross. He took the shame, the humiliation, the pain, all for us. With such an amazing example, how could we possibly act selfishly or out of conceit? May we follow that amazing example every day of our lives. Amen.

NIGHTY-NIGHT!

If you lie down, you will not be afraid;
when you lie down, your sleep will be sweet.
PROVERBS 3:24 ESV

It's so hard to fall asleep when you're worried about things. Bills. Job deadlines. Obligations. Relationship problems. Fears and concerns, legitimate or illusive. Isn't it wonderful to know that God wants our sleep to be sweet? It can be, when we trust Him with the details of our lives. As you rest your head on the pillow, as your eyes drift shut, picture yourself handing over your concerns to Jesus. See Him taking them into His hands and holding them close to his heart. He will do that, you know. He longs for you to release your cares, your concerns, so that you can have blissful rest. Ah! Doesn't a good night's sleep sound wonderful?

Lord, I have to confess, I sometimes have trouble falling
asleep. It's not always easy with so many things tumbling
through my mind. Please show me how to release these
things into Your hands, Father, then give me
a good night's rest. Amen.

ACT. . .OR RE-ACT?

*Dear children, let us not love with words
or speech but with actions and in truth.*
1 JOHN 3:18 NIV

- -

Have you ever thought about the fact that actions and
reactions are two different things? When we "act" we
make deliberate, methodical decisions to do something.
Everything is carefully thought out and bathed in prayer.
When we "re-act," we move swiftly, usually without
thinking. Regrets often follow. It's important to think
before acting, which is why we've got to rid ourselves (as
much as possible) from re-actions. It's not easy, but with
the guidance of the Holy Spirit, it is possible. Deliberate,
kind actions will go a long way in showing people the
love of Christ. Quick, knee-jerk reactions go a long way
in destroying relationships. The only difference between
the two? Just one little prefix: *re-*. So, which will you be: an
actor, or a re-actor? It's a daily choice.

*Father, please guard our thoughts, our words and our
actions, and please forgive us for the times
when we react and hurt others. Amen.*

PAYBACK!

Do not repay evil with evil or insult with insult,
on the contrary, repay evil with blessing, because to this
you were called so that you may inherit a blessing.
1 PETER 3:9 NIV

How often are we tempted to get even with those who hurt us? It's difficult not to knee jerk and repay an eye for an eye, but that's the opposite of what the Lord wants of us. We're instructed by scripture not to use the payback method. In fact, we're promised a blessing if we refrain from knee jerking and hurting those who've hurt us. The problem is, it's so hard to think beyond the moment. We need to base our decisions, our reactions, on long-term strategies and goals, not what feels right at that moment. If we go with what feels right in the moment, we'll make a lot of unwise choices.

Father, we're on a learning curve! We don't want to repay
evil with evil or insult with insult. It's not always easy,
for sure, but so worth it. Lord, we want our family to be
known as grace-filled, not as knee-jerkers. Thanks for
teaching us patience, Father. It might take awhile,
but we won't give up. Amen.

VICTORY

*I am grateful that God always makes
it possible for Christ to lead us to victory.*
2 CORINTHIANS 2:14 CEV

Picture your family, marching off to battle. The enemy is
off in the distance. You can see them just beyond the hill.
They're armed and ready, tall and sturdy, arrows pointed
straight at you and confident smirks on their faces. Still,
you're not flinching. You are prepared for this battle,
inside and out. What causes you to face the enemy with
no fear? What keeps your feet marching forward? You
know a very important secret: You're not alone. The Lord
Himself goes before you. He is fighting on your behalf.
All you have to do is show up, trust Him, and keep those
feet moving, one in front of the other. When you do so,
He builds your confidence with His very presence. Yes,
battles will come, but you are already victorious in Him.

*We're so glad You go before us, Lord. Our family is
protected because of You. You lead and guide us, which
brings such comfort. We're not alone. What a relief! Amen.*

HE SUPPLIES OUR NEEDS

*And my God will meet all your needs according to the
riches of his glory in Christ Jesus.*
PHILIPPIANS 4:19 NIV

There's a big difference between the things our family
needs and the things the individual members of the
family want. We might want nicer clothes or a fancier car,
but what we need might be more time together or more
time in God's Word. No matter what our needs are today,
God is in the business of supplying them. We don't have
to wonder if He knows when we have a lack. He knows,
and He's already working to fill the void. He might not
fill it exactly the way we'd like, but His ways are higher
than ours. Many times we get something completely
different and then discover it's far better than anything
we might've imagined for ourselves. God will supply. If
you're struggling today, don't forget: He's already working
on it.

*Whew! Father, what a relief to know You see our family's
lack. You won't leave us this way, Lord. Thank You for
filling the void in Your own time and Your own way.
We trust You, Father, and can't wait to see what You
have planned for us. Amen.*

*No, dear brothers and sisters, I have not achieved it,
but I focus on this one thing: Forgetting the past and looking
forward to what lies ahead, I press on to reach the end of
the race and receive the heavenly prize for which God,
through Christ Jesus, is calling us.*
PHILIPPIANS 3:13–14 NLT

Forgetting the past. Is that really possible? It's especially
tough in a family environment because members of the
family often don't let you forget the things you did wrong
yesterday. Or the day before. Or the year before. If you
carefully examine this verse you find an interesting word:
focus. We might not fully achieve our goal of completely
forgetting yesterday, but our focus must remain on what
lies ahead so that we can press toward the goal. This is a
race, after all, and we'll never make progress if we're
already looking over our shoulder. So, a healthy family is
a family that focuses on the goal, not the problems from
days gone by. It's not easy, but it's so worth it.

*Father, thank You for this reminder that we must
hyper-focus on the things that matter to You.
We will only win this race if our eyes are on You. Amen.*

A CALM SPIRIT

Be angry, and yet do not sin;
do not let the sun go down on your anger.
EPHESIANS 4:26 NASB

- - - - - - - - - - - - - - -

Okay, admit it. . .staying calm, cool, and collected isn't
always easy, especially with so many family dynamics
going on at once. You want to react with grace and joy,
but it doesn't always happen. Sometimes tempers get
the best of us, even when we try so hard to keep them
under control. When we let our emotions spiral out of
control, we have to let God reel us back in. One way we
do this is by not going to bed angry. If we can calm down
before our head hits the pillow, if we can truly not let
the sun go down on our anger, then we'll face a happier
day tomorrow. And, in a family environment a happier
tomorrow is a very, very good thing.

Father, staying calm isn't always easy. And once the kettle
starts boiling, it's hard to cool things down afterward.
Thank You for giving us the desire to make things better
tomorrow. Help us not to go to bed angry so that
peace will reign in our household. Amen.

*For this reason I bow my knees before the Father,
from whom every family in heaven and on earth is named.*
EPHESIANS 3:14–15 ESV

Every family on earth is patterned after our relationship
with our heavenly Father. We're His kids, and He's our
Daddy! What an amazing thing to think about. He's
the ultimate Father, a miraculous blend of love, grace,
and discipline. If we ever wanted to know where we fit
in, in our own families, all we have to do is look at His
headship. Because He's the ultimate Dad, the perfect
Father, the One who leads, guides, and corrects, we can
learn from the way He gently leads us. He doesn't beat
us over the head when we get it wrong. Far from it! When
we recognize this, we can relax and just be His kids. We
don't have to perform for Him or try to be perfect. There
are lessons to be learned, and He will teach them, but they
will mold us into kiddos He can be proud of.

*Father, thank You for the way You love. Your discipline
has been seasoned with whispers of love. What grateful
children of the King we are! Amen.*

RUNNING OVER

*Give, and it shall be given unto you; good measure,
pressed down, and shaken together, and running over,
shall men give into your bosom.*
LUKE 6:38 KJV

Picture a dry sponge dipped in water. When you lift it
out of the liquid, it's soaked clear through. In fact, if you
squeezed it, more water would come pouring out. It's
running over with moisture. That's exactly how it is when
we give. We're like a sponge, being dipped into the water.
God wants us to be filled so that we can give of ourselves,
then be refilled to give again. Over and over the process
goes, being filled, giving out, being filled, giving out.
There's such joy in sharing, after all! What a blessing to
give. So, the next time you're feeling blessed, take hold of
the concept that you've been blessed to be a blessing to
others, to share the joy and the provision so that others
can participate!

*Father, show us others that we can bless today. We want to
lead by example and bless them so that they can, in turn,
bless others. We will look for divine appointments! Amen.*

I will be careful to live an innocent life.
When will you come to me? I will live an innocent life
in my house. I will not look at anything wicked.
PSALM 101:2–3 NCV

What does it mean to live a life of purity? The word is most often used in association with sexual behavior, but there's far more to it than that. Purity and innocence go hand in hand. When you live a life of innocence, you're living proof that you can be in the world but not of the world. You understand the words "godly boundaries" and live within them. Of course, purity begins in the mind and heart. If our thoughts aren't pure, if our heart isn't settled on living a life of purity, then our actions will be skewed. We can't control externally what hasn't been confirmed internally, after all. So, guard your heart. Take your thoughts captive. Focus on Christ and commit yourself to walk in the ways He has set before you, completely pure and innocent.

We want pure, innocent hearts, Lord. We commit ourselves
to You afresh today and ask You to take captive our
thoughts, so that we can focus solely on what is good,
lovely, and pure. Amen.

*I will be glad and rejoice in you; I will sing
the praises of your name, O Most High.*
PSALM 9:2 NIV

We are called to lift a song of praise, even in the hardest
of times. As a family, we go through "tough stuff" (illness,
job loss, death of loved ones). It's hard to praise our way
through. But when we lift our hearts—and our eyes—we're
reminded that God is in control. We are encouraged by
the Word to give thanks "in all things." That means, even
when we're in a hard place, we still need to praise Him,
not just in song, but with our prayers. From the deepest
places in our hearts we must somehow—in spite of the
pain—look heavenward for answers, not inside ourselves.
Only God can mend what's truly broken, and He begins
that process when we open our mouths and usher forth
songs of praise.

*Things around us might not be perfect, but we can
battle in praise, Father. That's how we choose to live
our lives, completely immersed in a song of praise,
straight from our hearts to Yours! Amen.*

GOOD GIFTS

"If you, then, though you are evil, know how to give good gifts to your children, how much more will your Father in heaven give good gifts to those who ask him!"
MATTHEW 7:11 NIV

- - - - - - - - - - - - - - - - - - - -

Imagine it's your birthday. Your parents have told you they're going to give you money to spend on yourself. They drive you to the store and you head straight to the toy department, ready to spend, spend, spend. Then your mother opens up her purse and pulls out. . .a nickel. Just a nickel. "Don't spend it all in one place!" she says. You stare at the nickel and then back up at her. Is this a joke? Fortunately, it turns out to be. She gives you a wink, reaches back into her purse, and pulls out a twenty-dollar bill. Now we're talking! You dive in, buying just the right toy. Maybe this analogy is a little silly, but you get the idea. If parents know how to give their kids great gifts, why do we doubt that the Lord will go above and beyond? All we have to do (just check out the scripture above!) is ask.

We need Your blessings to shower down on us, Father. Please replace the things the enemy has stolen in our lives and give us all we need so that we can be a blessing to others. Amen.

I can do all things through him who strengthens me.
PHILIPPIANS 4:13 ESV

All things. Can you picture yourself, your family members, capable of doing all things? Impossible things? Daring things? Frightening things? It's true! When you're operating in the strength of the Lord, you are capable of the supernatural! That means His internal strength gives you everything you need to fight lions and bears with your bare hands, to toss rocks with slingshots at your Goliaths, and to walk across the sea with waters parted on both sides. Sound impossible? All of these things and more happened to real people who trusted in the Lord. They believed that God would strengthen them to do all things. . .and He did! Here's the challenge of the day: Can you trust Him to do supernatural things through you? Why not give it a try?

Father, We're excited to think that You want to do supernatural things through us. We can't wait to see what You have in store. We submit ourselves to You today, Lord, and wait in anticipation to see what You've got up Your sleeve. It's going to be great! Amen.

HATED. . .BUT BLESSED

Blessed are you when people hate you, when they exclude
you and insult you and reject your name as evil,
because of the Son of Man.
LUKE 6:22 NIV

People can be so mean! They mock and even reject us,
often because of our beliefs. They insult us and kick dirt
in our faces, just to prove a point. We will have to face
hatred and rejection in this life, as Jesus did, but how
do we respond? With more hatred? More anger? More
rejection? No, the Word of God is clear: We are to bless
those who hate us. Turn the other cheek. Show love, grace,
and mercy. This doesn't mean we should be a doormat.
Even Jesus flipped a few tables upside down in the
temple when the timing was right to do so. But more often
than not we simply have to forgive and come to grips with
the fact that some people simply aren't meant to be in our
inner circle. . .and that's okay.

Today we ask that You bless those who hurt,
insulted, and rejected us, Father. May You touch
their hearts as only You can. Amen.

A BLESSED FAMILY

The righteous lead blameless lives;
blessed are their children after them.
PROVERBS 20:7 NIV

Our family is blessed! Oh, what a wonderful thought. We're not held back or limited. All of God's blessings are ours in Christ. And this blessing travels down to our children, our grandchildren, and so on. To be blessed means we have unmerited favor (favor we didn't earn with our righteous acts). Aren't you glad you don't have to earn it? Yes, God calls us to live blameless lives, but it's the blood of Jesus, His sacrifice on the cross, that makes that possible. When we accept Him as Lord and Savior, our sins are washed away and we are made clean, blameless. And the blessings begin to flow, from us to our other family members. Oh, but how wonderful it is to be grateful for it and to live a life of gratitude!

We're blessed, Father! You've given us so much and increased our territory. Thank You for the work of Your Son on the cross so that we could obtain favor and blessing in our lives. We're beyond grateful, Lord. Amen.

ENDURANCE

*For everything that was written in the past was
written to teach us, so that through the endurance
taught in the Scriptures and the encouragement
they provide we might have hope.*
ROMANS 15:4 NIV

What a fascinating verse! We're taught that life is a race
and we've got to set our eye on the prize. But even the
most diligent runner can tell you that weariness will
set in when the race is underway. When we reach the
"giving up" point we've got to endure. Hang on. Dig
in our heels. Keep running, even when we feel we can't
catch our breath. Where does the courage to do this come
from? From our heavenly Father and from His Word. The
scriptures give us encouragement (courage) to keep going,
even when we don't feel like it. What hope we find in those
awesome verses! And that hope helps us put one foot in
front of the other, diligently running until the race is ended.

*Lord, we thank You for the reminder that even the best
trained runner gets weary. We see that encouragement
comes from You and from Your Word. When we get tired—
and we surely will—remind us to seek answers where the
only real answers can be found: in You. Amen.*

FAITH

*By faith the walls of Jericho fell, after the army had
marched around them for seven days.*
HEBREWS 11:30 NIV

- - - - - - - - - - - - - - - - - - - -

Seven days. That's how long the people of God marched
around the walls of Jericho. Seven days of hoping. Seven
days of praying. Seven days of believing. Seven days of
(possibly) doubting but doing their best to push those
doubts aside. At the end of those seven days, the walls
came tumbling down. Surely the people of God must've
celebrated! Their diligence paid off. Their faith was
rewarded. What a lesson we can learn from their example.
Our faith must remain strong, no matter how long or
how difficult the journey. We can't give up. We must keep
believing, keep hoping, keep our trust strong. Like those
Israelites, we will surely see the walls come tumbling down!

*Oh Lord, thank You! Thank You for this amazing example of
faith and tenacity. We want to be like the children of Israel
who trusted You, even in the face of the seemingly impossible.
May we keep marching, keep hoping, keep believing,
no matter how long it takes. Praise You, Father! Amen.*

*Stop all your dirty talk. Say the right thing at
the right time and help others by what you say.*
EPHESIANS 4:29 CEV

Dirty talk? What's that? Does this scripture refer to curse
words, or is there something more to be learned from this
verse? Sometimes dirty talk is talk that makes people
feel dirty afterwards. Perhaps there's no cursing at all.
Maybe it's just a conversation where you leave feeling
discouraged or hopeless because a friend dumped all
sorts of dirt on you. Or maybe it's a conversation where
you leave feeling guilty because you got pulled into a
gossip session. God longs for our conversations to be
pure and blameless. We've got to guard our words, and
not just the four-letter ones. When we say the right thing
at the right time, we lift people up. Say the wrong thing
at the right time—is there ever a right time for the wrong
words?—and we threaten to leave people covered in dirt.

*Lord, we want to leave people feeling good—about
themselves and You. We don't want to sling dirt, Father.
May our words be pure and blameless so that we bring honor
to You and build healthy relationships with others. Amen.*

My Christian brothers, you should be happy
when you have all kinds of tests. You know these
prove your faith. It helps you not to give up.
JAMES 1:2–3 NLV

Speed bumps. Ugh! They drive you crazy when you're
trying to get from Point A to Point B. They slow you
down. You have to keep tapping on the brake to keep the
car from jumping and jerking. On the other hand, speed
bumps serve a purpose. They protect the people who live
on that street by deliberately slowing down the traffic.
Sure, they might present an obstacle to the driver, but
to the homeowner, they're a blessing. Maybe it's time we
looked at our spiritual speed bumps through this same
lens. The little bumps in the road might be annoyances
in the moment, but perhaps they serve a greater purpose.
Maybe—just maybe—they're teaching us to persevere.
Maybe they're building our faith. Only time will tell. In
the meantime, look out! There's a speed bump ahead!

Lord, we don't really care for speed bumps. They're so
annoying. But we get it. You need to slow us down at times,
to protect us or others. Thanks for the reminder that they
serve a greater purpose, Father. We trust You, Lord. Amen.

A QUIET PLACE

At daybreak, Jesus went out to a solitary place.
LUKE 4:42 NIV

- -

A solitary place. Jesus retreated to a place apart from the others in His group so that He could be alone with His Father, and He want us to do the same. In the family environment this isn't always easy. Maybe you wish you could go to a solitary place but it feels impossible. You can't even go to the bathroom or take a shower without someone beating on the door. Today, look for opportunities to set yourself apart with the Lord for some quiet time, even if it means you have to close your door to accomplish it. He longs to spend time with you. . .in the stillness. That means we have to press aside any anxieties or racing thoughts and focus solely on Him. It's not easy, but Jesus—our great example—showed us that time alone with Daddy God is critical to a great relationship with Him.

Father, thank You for wooing us into a secret place with You. We each need those set-apart times, Lord. They're not always easy to find, but when we're with You all of our cares and concerns disappear. We praise You, Lord, for drawing us by Your Spirit. Amen.

Dear brothers and sisters, honor those who are your leaders in the Lord's work. They work hard among you and give you spiritual guidance.
1 Thessalonians 5:12 nlt

- - - - - - - - - - - - - - - - - - - -

We are commanded in scripture to honor those who are our leaders in the Lord's work. A workman is worth his hire, so the first way we honor them is by making sure their basic needs are met. Next, we honor them with our words. Even when we disagree, we give the benefit of the doubt until proven otherwise. So many times our pastors, worship leaders, and so forth are picked apart by church members. How painful it must be, to give your life in service to God, only to be attacked. Remember to pray for your pastors and church leaders. And offer to help. Volunteer as much as you're able. Be known as a family that loves and supports their leaders. God will honor these choices.

Lord, we're glad You reminded us to pray for those in spiritual leadership. They work so hard. No, they don't always get it right, but we can pray and encourage, all the same. Thank You, Father, for those You've placed as leaders in Your work. Amen.

A PRAISING FAMILY

And at midnight Paul and Silas prayed, and sang praises
unto God: and the prisoners heard them.
ACTS 16:25 KJV

When did Paul and Silas pray? In the midnight hour!
They chose the very moment when things were darkest
to sing a worship song. Did they sing them quietly? No
way! Perhaps you've heard the phrase "at the top of their
lungs." It definitely applies in this case. Their praising
was so loud it woke the other prisoners (and eventually
set them free). Can you imagine singing with such
boisterous praise while in prison? We have a hard time
ushering up a few words of praise when we're having
a bad day! But boisterous praise breaks chains. It sets
prisoners free. So, dare to praise at the top of your lungs.
Sing a song to God in the very middle of your toughest
circumstance. Then watch as He sets you—and your
family—free from the things that have held you bound.

We long to be set free, Father! So we choose to praise You.
You are worthy of our praise, no matter what we're going
through. You are our King, our Lord, our Savior, and we
worship You because of who You are. Praise You, Lord. Amen.

CONFESSION IS GOOD FOR THE SOUL

*If we confess our sins, he is faithful and just to forgive us
our sins and to cleanse us from all unrighteousness.*
1 JOHN 1:9 ESV

- - - - - - - - - - - - - - - - - -

Why do you suppose God calls us to confess our sins
to Him? He knows that confession is (truly) good for
the soul. When we get things off our chest, we're free to
move forward. Perhaps you've struggled with this in your
family. Maybe people like to hang on to things instead of
confessing them. Small children, for example, will go on
saying, "It's her fault" instead of owning up to the truth.
Pointing the finger only divides. Confessing and dealing
with things—even when difficult—will bring healing. So,
why not have a confession day at your house? Invite
people to a safe place to make their confessions and then
watch as God works to forgive and heal.

*Today we confess our sins to You, Lord. We lay it all out
there, knowing You will choose to love us anyway and to
offer us a clean slate. Please help us to do this to others in
our family, Father. We all need a fresh start. Amen.*

*But Ruth said, "Do not urge me to leave you
or to return from following you. For where you go I will go,
and where you lodge I will lodge. Your people shall
be my people, and your God my God."*
RUTH 1:16 ESV

Don't you love the story of Ruth? Her words to her
mother-in-law, Naomi, have touched countless lives. She
committed herself to stick close to Naomi, but beyond
that, she made a commitment to stay connected to
Naomi's "people" (the family of God). It's the same with
us. God calls us to stay connected to other believers.
When we wander away from the fold we face dangers.
But when we stick close, when we make His people
our people, we're inside the safety net. Best of all, we're
surround by people who love us, who "get" us, and who
are like-minded. These are the people we get to do life
with. What a blessed privilege!

*We're so grateful for the people You've put in our lives,
Father. They're our family! We're brothers and sisters,
quick to lend support and to love one another through life's
storms. We feel so blessed to live in community with
like-minded people, Lord. Thank You for that! Amen.*

GOD, OUR ROCK

I find rest in God; only he can save me. He is my rock and my salvation. He is my defender; I will not be defeated.
PSALM 62:1–2 NCV

- -

Oftentimes we hear one spouse say of the other, "He's my rock" or "She's my rock." What they're really saying is, "He's the one I know I can go to when things around me are in chaos. He's steady. He's reliable." A rock is immovable. God is the true "rock" in our lives. He won't budge with circumstances. He won't drift away with heavy winds. He stays rooted. Grounded. Ready to hold our weight when we cling to Him. Today, no matter what your family is going through, look to God, your rock. Picture yourself swimming out, past the rocky seas, to that solid rock, then climbing up, up, up, to a cleft, where you rest. He's your safety, your defender. What a good God we have!

Father, You are our rock. You will not be moved, even when the earth around us is shaking and our lives are in transition. We can count on You, Lord. We run to You, cling to You, rest in You. Praise You for being there for us, through thick and thin. Amen.

I always thank my God as I remember you in my prayers.
PHILEMON 1:4 NIV

Have you ever pondered the word *always*? When you say you'll *always* do something, it means you won't walk away and forget. Unfortunately, we don't *always* remember to *always* do what we say. We're forgetful people! Aren't you glad God is an *always* God? He brings to mind the things we forget to remember, like praying for specific people at specific times. What an honor, to lift someone up in prayer as they're walking through tough situations. And how good of the Lord, to bring them to mind at just the right moment. Our prayers have a rebound effect, too. Those very people we're praying for are the ones who lift us up when we're in need. What a lovely prayer circle, and what a wonderful God, to remain at the center of it all.

I love our prayer circle, God. We're surrounded by people praying for us, and we pray for them as well. Thanks for bringing to mind the folks who need our prayers today. We lift them up to Your throne, grateful to have them in our lives. Amen.

Whoever brings trouble on their family will inherit only
wind, and the fool will be servant to the wise.
PROVERBS 11:29 NIV

It's one thing for an outsider to bring trouble to the
family, another thing altogether for a family member
to stir up chaos from the inside. It's not just dangerous
for the family; it's dangerous for the individual doing
the stirring. Today's verse is really clear: A person who
brings trouble on his family will inherit the wind. What
does that mean, anyway? The wind blows here and there.
You can't grab hold of it. When you cause trouble for the
family, you're taking away your right to inherit anything
tangible. You'd rather grab hold of the wind than anything
the family has to offer. So, think carefully before you
create chaos in the home. If you're looking to hang on
to something sturdier than the wind, you might want to
reconsider before getting your family members riled up.

Help us when we're tempted to stir up trouble, Lord.
Calm our hearts and spirits and give us patience.
We each want to be examples to the others,
even during the tough times. Amen.

CHOOSE YOU THIS DAY

"But if serving the LORD seems undesirable to you,
then choose for yourselves this day whom you will serve,
whether the gods your ancestors served beyond the Euphrates,
or the gods of the Amorites, in whose land you are living.
But as for me and my household, we will serve the LORD."
JOSHUA 24:15 NIV

Every single day we have to make a choice to serve the Lord. For some, the idea of walking the straight and narrow seems too confining. They choose not to serve Him. But, as for our house, we can—and will—choose to keep God first and foremost, in our home, our hearts, and our giftings. He will maintain the proper place as long as we allow Him to. Serving Him isn't cumbersome. It's a blessing. It's not confining. It's freeing! In fact, dedicating our family to God is the safest thing we can do. It's a daily choice, sure, but one we will never regret making.

Lord, today we choose to put You first in our home.
You won't be an afterthought. You won't be a
"maybe if nothing else works out." We're all in, Father.
You're the head of this household, and we will serve
You all the days of our lives. Amen.

He has made everything beautiful in its time. He has also set eternity in the human heart; yet no one can fathom what God has done from beginning to end.
ECCLESIASTES 3:11 NIV

It's difficult to figure out the Lord's timetable. Perhaps that's because God isn't ruled by the clock. He's not on the 24-7 plan. To Him, a day is like a thousand years and a thousand years like a day. Perhaps that's why He's not bothered when answers to our prayers don't come instantaneously. He knows they're coming and isn't worried about when. We, on the other hand, are ruled by the clock. We want to know all of the specifics, especially the answer to the "when?" question. We need to remember that God makes all things beautiful in His time, not our time. When we settle into the peace of that statement, it changes everything. We can't fathom how wonderful the outcome will be, but we can trust Him with it. . .in His time. Until then, we remain faithful, even when it's difficult.

Lord, remind us daily that we don't need to be ruled by the clock. The only thing that matters is Your love and faithfulness. Amen.

A SACRIFICE OF PRAISE

Is any among you afflicted? let him pray.
Is any merry? let him sing psalms.
JAMES 5:13 KJV

The cure for what ails us is always the same: praise and thanksgiving. When we offer up a song of praise we're lifted above our circumstances, into a heavenly realm. In that lofty place we lose all recollection of the troubles below. For those moments, we're elevated above our troubles. The reason it's called a *sacrifice* is because it doesn't always come naturally, or easily. To sacrifice means we do it anyway, even if it's painful. The cool thing about praise, though, is that once you get started, it's no longer difficult! So, lift your heart. Lift your voice. Lift a song. Then watch as God takes those afflictions, those things that are nagging you, and shifts your focus from your troubles to pure joy.

We offer a sacrifice of praise, Lord. It's not always easy, but it's a choice we make because we know the outcome is always good. We love spending time in Your presence. That's where healing comes. So here we come, Father! We're happy to lift our voices to You! Amen.

HERE, LITTLE SHEEP!

*"What do you think? If a man owns a hundred sheep,
and one of them wanders away, will he not leave
the ninety-nine on the hills and go to look
for the one that wandered off?"*
MATTHEW 18:12 NIV

- -

Aren't you glad the Lord comes looking for us when
we wander away? He doesn't leave us for the wolves to
devour. Even if it means leaving the other sheep in the
field He searches until He locates us. He cares that much.
You wouldn't think He would notice one little sheep,
wandering away from the fold, but He does. His level of
caring goes above and beyond, and He doesn't give up
on us, even if we wander more than once. He just keeps
looking for us, hoping we'll submit ourselves to His
leadership, His will. Once we learn to place our trust in
Him we're happy to stay in the fold. In that place we're
completely safe, totally cared for. Now that's a very good
shepherd!

*Father, we have a tendency to wander and find ourselves
in trouble. The wolves are perched and ready to snatch us,
but You always arrive just in time, ready to carry us back
to the fold. We're so grateful, Lord. Amen.*

All hard work brings a profit,
but mere talk leads only to poverty.
PROVERBS 14:23 NIV

Why is it that the right thing is usually the hard thing?
The very things we're supposed to be doing are usually
the things we don't want to do. Take housekeeping, for
instance. Or laundry. These tasks don't always come
naturally, but if we want to succeed, if we want to profit,
we must work hard. We can talk all day about the work
we need to do—go grocery shopping, mop the floors, pay
the bills, organize the closets—but the work isn't going to
get done on its own. We have to dedicate ourselves, then
dive in. And, isn't it wonderful, on the other side of the
task? Looking at a clean house, an organized closet, a full
pantry. . .these things are blissful.

Lord, sometimes we need a burst of energy. We need our
"want to" back. You're great at stirring us to action, Father,
so we're counting on You to help us not only get started,
but get the job done. With Your help we can do it. Amen.

MONEY

The love of money causes all kinds of trouble. Some people
want money so much that they have given up their faith
and caused themselves a lot of pain.

1 TIMOTHY 6:10 CEV

Perhaps you've heard it quoted that money is the root of
all evil. That's completely untrue. Money, in and of itself,
isn't evil at all. It's neutral. We get into trouble when we
fall in love with money, when we pursue it above more
important things. When we do this, we often get hyper-
focused on financial gain and forget all about our faith
walk. We tread on dangerous ground. The love of money
causes all kinds of trouble, and it's hard to clean up the
damage after-the-fact. Love (unlike money) isn't neutral.
It's a driving force. So when you love money, you're
driven. You want more, and more, and more. You never
have enough. You're never satisfied. And dissatisfaction
is the enemy of God. So, guard your heart and learn to be
content with what you have. May money never become
the object of your passion.

Father, thanks for the reminder that our pursuit of money—
and material possessions—pulls us away from You.
We commit to keep You in Your rightful place, Lord. Amen.

A wise son brings joy to his father,
but a foolish man despises his mother.
PROVERBS 15:20 NIV

- -

How is it possible that so many different personalities exist in one family? One child is diligent and kind, the other is foolish and self-seeking. It makes no sense! Joy and pain exist side-by-side causing emotions to swing back and forth from day to day. Some would point to the parenting and say Mom and Dad are responsible for the foolish child. They would speculate that the self-seeking child has been spoiled. Oftentimes this isn't the case at all; it's just a matter of varying personalities. No matter how many family dynamics you're facing, you can get through it. God can still be honored. It means sticking to your guns and offering tough love, but it will be worth it, for the whole family.

Lord, with joy and pain living side by side in our house,
our emotions run the gamut. Just about the time we think
we've got a handle on things, the pendulum swings the
other way. Today we're asking You to help us live
in balance. Only You can accomplish this, Father.
We thank You in advance. Amen.

But let all who take refuge in you be glad; let them ever sing for joy. Spread your protection over them, that those who love your name may rejoice in you.
PSALM 5:11 NIV

Can you imagine going out in a storm without an umbrella? You'd be soaked in a hurry! The Bible tells us that the Lord spreads His protection over us. We have to think of that like an umbrella. When the storms of life blow in, His covering is there. We can dance and sing underneath that holy umbrella because we know we're safe. We also know that He's right there, so close we could practically reach out and grab hold of His hand. And God's protection extends to the whole family. There's none too old or too young. He covers us all. We take refuge in Him during the storm, but more than that. . .we praise Him in the storms. Praising is easy to do when we've got the assurance that He has everything taken care of.

Lord, we're glad You're our umbrella during the storms of life. We trust You, Father. You've got us completely covered, and we can dance and sing and praise our way through. That's what we choose to do today, Lord. Amen!

*Therefore my heart is glad and my tongue rejoices;
my body also will rest secure.*
PSALM 16:9 NIV

- -

When our hearts are happy, our physical bodies respond
in a positive way. Our heart rate calms down. Our
troubling thoughts vanish. Our breathing steadies.
Happiness is contagious! It's affective. And it just doesn't
affect us. The smile on our face is contagious to those
around us. They see our lips curled up in a smile and
respond with a grin. And on and on it goes. It all starts
with one happy heart. Best of all, we can rest secure when
our hearts are happy, because a happy heart is a heart
that's fully committed to trusting God, no matter what.
So what are you waiting for? C'mon! Get happy!

*Lord, we get it! Our bodies are waiting for our hearts to be
happy. Once that happens, our bodies will respond. Fill our
hearts with Your joy today, Father. We want to be contagious
so that others can share in the happiness. Amen.*

THE GOOD SAMARITAN

Jesus replied, "A man was going down from Jerusalem to Jericho, and he fell among robbers, who stripped him and beat him and departed, leaving him half dead."
LUKE 10:30 ESV

The story of the Good Samaritan grabs hold of our hearts every time. Our hearts go out to the poor man who fell among thieves and was robbed and beaten. Then we get angry at all of the people who passed by and didn't offer to help. Finally, we breathe a sigh of relief as the Samaritan—the least likely person—not only offers to help, but goes above and beyond the call of duty. We see ourselves in all of these characters, but the one we should strive to be most like is the one who stopped to offer assistance. Our prayer, as a family, should be to care for others in need, like the Good Samaritan. When others look at our family, may they see us as people who genuinely care for those in need and stop to lend a hand.

Father, we love this story. We feel so bad for the man who was injured. We've been in his shoes. We long to be more like the Good Samaritan, the one who stopped and lent a hand. Show us how to minister to those in need. Amen.

For I am convinced that neither death nor life,
neither angels nor demons, neither the present nor the future,
nor any powers, neither height nor depth, nor anything else in
all creation, will be able to separate us from the love
of God that is in Christ Jesus our Lord
ROMANS 8:38-39 NIV

Have you ever tried to untie a knot that refused to budge?
If so, you have some idea how difficult it would be for
someone—or something—to pluck you from God's hand.
The two of you are tightly knit together and nothing can
pull you apart. Problems may come, but nothing is strong
enough to yank you from God's hand. No relational crisis,
no job loss, no illness, no financial windfall, no great
success, no huge failure. . .nothing can separate you from
the love of God. Whew! Knowing this offers a huge sense
of relief. We don't have to earn His love. Even now, He's
drawing you close, whispering in your ear, and working
on your behalf. . .whether you've had a good day or bad.
Whether you're up or down. He adores you. Period.

We're so relieved, Lord! You adore us, and nothing can
separate us from Your love. We can breathe
a sigh of relief, knowing we're Yours. Amen.

TEMPER

*But now also put these things out of your life: anger,
bad temper, doing or saying things to hurt others,
and using evil words when you talk.*
COLOSSIANS 3:8 NCV

Temper, temper! Those of us who struggle with anger
often hear these words. Dealing with a bad temper isn't
just a childhood problem; it's something we struggle
with. . .forever. This can be quite a challenge in a family
setting with so many people living together. Imagine how
crazy it would be if everyone got mad at the same time.
Fiasco! No, it's better to count to ten, release a slow breath,
then ask God to remove the anger from you. And He can
take it if you come out swinging. Don't ever be afraid to let
your emotions show with the Lord. He created you, after
all. He certainly knows when you're emotional! But do your
best to calm down, quiet your spirit, and offer forgiveness.
When you do so, you're less likely to hurt others.

*Lord, please guard our hearts! We give You our emotions,
Father. We release our anger into Your hands
and ask for peace in its place. Amen.*

Dear friend, do not imitate what is evil but what is good.
Anyone who does what is good is from God.
Anyone who does what is evil has not seen God.
3 JOHN 1:11 NIV

- -

How do babies learn how to walk? To talk? To sing? They imitate their parents! How do children learn to write, to do math, to take tests? They imitate their teachers. How do musicians learn to play piano, violin, and so forth? They imitate their instructors. All of life is an opportunity to mimic those around us so that we can grow. Because we have this innate desire to be like others, it's very important to pay attention to what we mimic. We've got to be careful to imitate only what is good, not what is evil. So, if you're going to be a copycat—and we all are, to some extent—just make sure you're copying holy behaviors, not evil ones.

Lord, I guess it's true. . .we're all imitators. More than anything, we want to imitate You. We long to be like You, Father. May we be known for our purity, our holiness. May evil flee from us. Thank You for being the ultimate example, Lord. Amen.

Do not be anxious about anything, but in every situation,
by prayer and petition, with thanksgiving,
present your requests to God.
PHILIPPIANS 4:6 NIV

There's something about lifting our needs to God that's very freeing. The very act of lifting our arms in surrender makes us feel better. Problems vanish. Weights are lifted. Of course, it's easier to release our anxieties when our arms aren't tightly wrapped around them, so we have to be willing to let go. It's a choice. Whatever anxieties you're hanging on to today, make a conscious decision to release them into the Lord's hands. He's the only one capable of dealing with them, and you'll be thrilled to see just how much lighter your load is once the burdens are lifted. What are you waiting for? Lift those arms and feel them release!

Lord, we don't like feeling anxious. Anxiety wraps itself
around our hearts and squeezes until we can't breathe.
We're giving You our burdens and anxieties today, Father.
Thank You for lifting them and freeing us up! Amen.

For God is not a God of confusion but of peace,
as in all the churches of the saints.
1 CORINTHIANS 14:33 ESV

God doesn't stir up confusion. It's important to know this because we're often confused and wonder if God is behind it. He's not. The enemy of our souls is the author of confusion. The Lord is light, guiding our path. So, if you are facing confusion today—as an individual or a family—first come to grips with the fact that God isn't behind it. Speak the name of Jesus and take a stand against the enemy. He has to flee, along with any confusing thoughts, at that name. God is a peace-giver, not a chaos-giver. What a relief!

Father, we thank You for the reminder that You're
not the one creating confusing, chaotic thoughts
in our minds. We command those thoughts
to go, in Jesus' name! Amen.

"Salvation is found in no one else,
for there is no other name under heaven given
to mankind by which we must be saved."
ACTS 4:12 NIV

There's no other name given to us than the name of Jesus. It's the name above all names and the only one by which we can be saved. When we call on Jesus, He delivers us out of darkness, out of the pits we're in, and places our feet on higher ground. We can try all day, but no other name we call on has that kind of power. People call on the name of money and it doesn't save. They call on relationships. Relationships don't save. They call out, "Family!" But even family doesn't save. Only one name has that kind of power. So why not call on the name of Jesus today?

Jesus, Jesus, Jesus! There's truly something special about that name, Lord! When we call on the name of Jesus, demons have to flee! Through that amazing name our lives have been changed. We've been saved, set free. How can we ever thank You enough for sending Your Son, Father. Amen!

ATTITUDE

Those who live according to the flesh have their minds
set on what the flesh desires; but those who live
in accordance with the Spirit have their minds
set on what the Spirit desires.
ROMANS 8:5 NIV

- -

We are governed (driven) by our nature. If our nature is evil, then our actions will follow. If our nature is reborn of the spirit, then positive actions follow. Isn't it wonderful to know that we don't have to try to recreate our own spirits or to work hard at getting things right once we're in relationship with Christ? On the contrary! The very act of asking Jesus to live in our hearts serves as the catalyst for change. And what a change! Our entire nature is reborn. Even the more dangerous criminal, once born of the Spirit, has a godly nature. What an amazing, transforming God we serve.

You've changed our nature, God! We're not who we used to
be. Our thoughts, reactions, and attitudes are completely
different. And You're no respecter of persons. What You've
done for us, You'll do for others. Thank You for Your
transforming power, Father! Amen.

FAVORITISM

My friends, if you have faith in our glorious Lord Jesus
Christ, you won't treat some people better than others.
JAMES 2:1 CEV

Most of us would argue that we don't play favorites, but
is that really the case? There are so many ways we show
favoritism, and many times we don't even realize we're
doing it. We overlook one friend to talk to another. We
walk past one child to gloat about another. We prefer one
co-worker's company to another. It happens all the time. It's
hard enough when people who don't know the Lord behave
like this, but when Christians do it, it breaks the Lord's
heart. He doesn't want us to treat others preferentially.
Why? Because He adores us all. . .equally. He treats
every single one the same. We're all His favorites. So pay
attention. Make sure you're not overlooking some of His
kids and preferring others. Don't play favorites!

Lord, we're closer to some friends than others, and we
know that's not really the problem. The real problem is,
we choose to deliberately ignore some people. They just aren't
on our radar. Thanks for putting them back on, Father.
And thanks for putting them in our lives. Amen.

And this gospel of the kingdom shall be preached in all the world for a witness unto all nations.
MATTHEW 24:14 KJV

How is it possible for one family to reach the nations? Does God want us to travel to South America? Africa? Europe? If so, should we become full-time missionaries? The truth is, not everyone is called to a life of full-time missions work. That's not what this scripture refers to, anyway. We're called to be salt and light, to minister to people around us, no matter where we are. Whether we're in the city, the country, the suburbs, or traveling abroad, we have to let our lights shine bright. And we have to be ready to share the Gospel at any moment. The Lord might send someone directly into our path today, perhaps the lady next door or a friend in school. If our lights are shining brightly, we're doing our part to reach the nations, right where we are.

Lord, we love the idea of going on a missions trip, but we also love the idea that You can use us—our whole family—right where we are. Thanks for that privilege, Father. May our lights shine bright for You. Amen.

THE BEST YOU CAN

In all the work you are doing, work the best you can.
Work as if you were doing it for the Lord, not for people.
COLOSSIANS 3:23 NCV

- - - - - - - - - - - - - - - - - - - -

All our lives we've heard the phrases, "Give it your all!"
"Do the best you can!" And so, we do. We give it our all in
school. We do the best we can in sports. We fight to climb
the corporate ladder at work. We throw our very lives into
raising our children. We give, give, give, and yet somehow
still come out feeling like we're not doing enough. How
is this possible? We need to remember that all we do has
to be "as unto the Lord." It's for Him. When we see God
as the recipient of our work, it puts a whole new spin on
things. Our schoolwork? It's for Him! Our parenting? It's
for Him. Our dedication on the job? It's for Him.

Father, I'm tired of feeling like I'm not good enough.
I give and give and come up short.
Thank You for the reminder that
my work is for You, not others. Amen.

WORSHIP

Come, let us bow down in worship,
let us kneel before the L ORD our Maker.
PSALM 95:6 NIV

What does it mean to bow down in worship? Does this verse refer to a literal position, or is there something more to be taken from it? To bow the knee to God means to surrender. When we kneel to Him we're saying, "Your will, not mine." A true heart of worship surrenders itself to God's will in every area, even when things don't make sense. Yes, we can literally bow the knee, but when our hearts are bowed, when our minds are bowed, then we're truly in worship. We aren't seeking our own way. We're praising and worshiping the One who knows a better way, a higher way, a more beneficial way. Humbling yourself on your knees might seem a lowly act, but it's the highest possible form of praise.

Father, we bow the knee to You today! We want Your will
to be done in our lives. We come to You with submitted
hearts and minds, ready for a higher perspective.
May Your will be done, we pray. Amen.

*He that hath an ear, let him hear what the Spirit
saith unto the churches.*
REVELATION 2:17 KJV

- - - - - - - - - - - - - - - - - -

The Holy Spirit is our Comforter and Friend. He's
also whispering in our ear, giving direction, guidance,
comfort. The problem is, we don't always hear what
He's saying because we're so distracted by the chaos of
the world around us. God wants us to have "an ear to
hear." What He's really saying is, "Pay attention!" When
we pay attention, we're tuned in. We're anticipating.
Waiting. Focused. We want to know what's going to be
said (or done) next. The Holy Spirit is speaking. Are you
listening?

*Lord, thank You for Your sweet, precious Spirit. So many
times we've needed a special word or a little nudge and
there it is. . .that still, small voice. We're so honored that
You would speak to us, Lord. May we tune out every
distraction so we can remain focused on what You're
saying, Father. We're listening. Amen.*

BROTHERLY LOVE

Behold, how good and how pleasant it is for
brothers to dwell together in unity!
PSALM 133:1 NASB

- - - - - - - - - - - - - - - - - - - -

Most of us who reside with family members might rewrite this verse to say "how good and pleasant it is for brothers and sisters to dwell together in unity!" Siblings don't always get along. Sometimes the bickering can go on for hours and drive people crazy. It is possible to slow down the arguing, and it all comes down to one word: *unity*. When we're unified, when we all feel like part of a larger team instead of random individuals thrown together in the same house, we work toward the same goals. We want a unified outcome. We're not looking out for number one; we're seeking what's best for the group. So, the best way you can pray for your family today is to say, "Lord, unify us!" He will of course! He's in the business of unifying.

Father, we're so glad You're our unifier. You can bring
even the most unique individuals together as one team.
Only by Your Spirit is this possible, Lord. We're so grateful
that You see our family as one big happy team, Father.
Thanks for holding us together! Amen.

TIME MANAGEMENT

Look carefully then how you walk, not as unwise but as wise, making the best use of the time, because the days are evil. Therefore do not be foolish, but understand what the will of the Lord is.
EPHESIANS 5:15–17 ESV

We all want to be better at managing our time. One way to do that is to take the temperature test. Take your temperature every two hours over a twenty-four hour period. According to one theory, we are at our peak when our temperature is at its highest (even if it's just an nth of a degree). Once you know your peak time you can schedule things around it. This works great in a family, too. Sure, different people will peak at different times but imagine how helpful this will be when you're setting up a chores chart! You'll make the best possible use of everyone's time and the work will get done in the process.

Father, You created us. You know when we work best, whether it's morning, noon, or night. We want to be better at managing our time, Lord. Please help us in this area so that we can accomplish more for Your kingdom. Amen.

As for you, you meant evil against me, but God meant it for good in order to bring about this present result, to preserve many people alive.
GENESIS 50:20 NASB

Life isn't fair. We need to acknowledge that up front. Bad things happen to good people. The Bible is loaded with stories of people who took the fall for others: Think of Joseph, for instance. He was thrown into a pit and sold into slavery by his own brothers! Perhaps the greatest "unfair" story of all is the one that has the potential to change all of our lives. Was it fair that Jesus Christ, who never sinned, had to go to the cross for us? Fair? No. Was He willing? Yes. You see, enduring the "unfair" moments in life often has powerful results on the other side. So don't argue when unfair things happen. Just pray that God will redeem them and turn them around for His glory.

Lord, You took on our sin and shame on the cross.
May we learn to bear the "not fair" moments
in our lives with such grace! Amen.

For this reason, I ask you to keep using the gift God gave
you. It came to you when I laid my hands on you and
prayed that God would use you.
2 TIMOTHY 1:6 NLV

God gives us gifts for a reason. They're meant to be
used for Him. In a family environment, there are often
many gifts working in tandem. Spiritual gifts. Artistic
gifts. Academic gifts. Perhaps one is good on the piano.
Another is a solid writer. Another is a gifted speaker or
teacher. All of these can work together to help get the
Gospel message out. And remember, God doesn't take
those gifts away from us. He wants us to keep polishing
them (exercising them) so that they're useable for years to
come. There's no point in saying, "Oh, I used to sing but
now I don't." Why not take it up again? You never know!
God just might use you to minister directly to someone's
heart with your song.

Lord, I'll be the first to admit I don't pay as much attention
to my gifts (artistic, academic, or spiritual) as I once did.
Today I lay those gifts at your feet as an offering. Show me
how I can use them to glorify You, Father. Amen.

STUFF

Do not love the world or anything in the world.
If anyone loves the world, the love of
the Father is not in him.
1 JOHN 2:15 NIV

- -

Our homes are filled with "stuff," some of it necessary, some of it not. We're overloaded. We can't turn around without bumping into (or tripping over) more stuff. And yet, the more we have, the more we want. We're conditioned by television commercials and magazine advertisements to buy, buy, buy. We've got to be careful with all of this stuff though. If we start to long for it more than we long for God, we're out of balance. All of the electronic goodies in the world don't come close to one moment spent with Him. So guard your heart. Maybe some of that stuff needs to be sold in a garage sale so there's room to kneel down and worship the giver of all good things.

Father, thanks for the reminder that You're the giver
of the things we really need. All we need is You, Lord.
We have enough stuff. May we focus on our
relationship with You, Father. Amen.

Commit your way to the LORD;
trust in him, and he will act.
PSALM 37:5 ESV

Not everyone has a stick-to-it attitude. Many try something, fail, drop it, and quickly try something else. Here's the problem with that: We often miss out on God's best because we didn't stick around long enough to figure out if it would work for us. We'd rather bounce, bounce, bounce from thing to thing, church to church, relationship to relationship. To be committed means you hang around long enough to give something an honest try. This is especially true when it comes to trusting God. We've got to stick with Him, even if it looks as if He's not going to come through. He will. . .but if we don't stick with Him, we might miss it when He moves. So, stay committed. Don't give up!

Lord, we want our whole family to be committed. We're not quitters, Father. We're going to hang in there as long as it takes. We trust You, Lord, and we will be watching when You come through for us. Amen.

SLOW TO SPEAK

Understand this, my dear brothers and sisters:
You must all be quick to listen, slow to speak,
and slow to get angry. Human anger does not
produce the righteousness God desires.
JAMES 1:19–20 NLT

- - - - - - - - - - - - - -

Have you ever taken a video and set it on slow motion?
It's fun to watch, isn't it? When you slow things down, you
notice everything: the shape of a person's mouth as they
speak. The way their legs move when they run. The funny
expressions, magnified. Oh, if only we had a way to slow
things down right before that moment when we open
our mouths to spout off at someone. If only someone
would hit the pause button so that we could think, think,
think before speaking. There might not be a literal pause
button, but the Holy Spirit will do this work for us if we
allow Him to. Next time you're about to give a quick
response to something. . .pause. Move in slow motion. Let
the Spirit of God have His way.

Lord, I'm so quick to say things, and I often end up
regretting them afterward. Thank You for slowing me
down, Father. Guard my mouth and my heart.
May I think before speaking, I pray. Amen.

"Who are you?" he asked. "I am your servant Ruth,"
she said. "Spread the corner of your garment over me,
since you are a guardian-redeemer of our family."
RUTH 3:9 NIV

The story of Ruth is a beautiful but sobering tale of a
young woman with no one to "cover" her. Other than her
mother-in-law, Naomi, she had no family of her own. But
she found herself in a strange land with unfamiliar people
and met a man named Boaz, a distant relative of Naomi's,
who "covered" her (both literally and figuratively) and
made her part of the family. Today, as we gather with
those we love, maybe we spread our family blanket out
to include those who have no families, those who are
lonely and wishing they had someone to talk to. Perhaps,
in doing so, our family will grow far beyond its current
borders to include a whole new set of members.

Lord, we know there are people who need family.
Elderly people. Young people. People we can sweep under
our wing. Show us when and how to spread the blanket to
these people, to draw them into the fold. Amen.

*"Therefore do not worry about tomorrow,
for tomorrow will worry about itself.
Each day has enough trouble of its own."*
MATTHEW 6:34 NIV

- -

Some people are afraid of the future. They're terrified of what it might hold. They worry about it before it even arrives. Others are hyper-focused on the future because they're disappointed with today. They're unhappy with their present circumstances and dream of better days ahead. There's nothing wrong with hoping for a happier tomorrow, but we shouldn't overlook what God is doing right now, right here. Perhaps He's moving in ways we can't see or understand. If we're too preoccupied on getting past today, we might just miss an amazing moment with Him. On the other hand, we shouldn't be afraid of the future either. We've got to trust that the Lord has all of our days in the palm of His hand: yesterday, today, and tomorrow.

Lord, we can trust You with our days. Maybe today isn't great. Maybe we've got some concerns about tomorrow. But we know You're trustworthy, Father, so we're hanging on to that. We're so grateful that You've got this! Amen.

*When the hour had come, He reclined at the table,
and the apostles with Him. And He said to them,
"I have earnestly desired to eat this Passover with you
before I suffer; for I say to you, I shall never again
eat it until it is fulfilled in the kingdom of God."*
LUKE 22:14–16 NASB

Jesus loved His disciples so much. One of His most
memorable times with them took place on the night
before His crucifixion when He gathered with them for
what is now called "The Last Supper." Gathering around
the table, He shared His heart. That's how it is with us,
too. We gather close around the table, not just to eat the
food that's been prepared, but to share our hearts. To
spend a few minutes unified, as a family. Deep things can
happen around a table, if we will let them. And, like that
holy night so long ago, Jesus is present, as long as we
invite Him to be.

*Lord, thank You for joining us around the table. We're so
grateful for the time we can spend as a family. Having You
there, in our midst, makes every meal a holy meal.
Talk about true table fellowship! Amen.*

"Can any one of you by worrying
add a single hour to your life?"
MATTHEW 6:27 NIV

We get so wrapped up with worry sometimes! And, when we live in a family, people start to worry in tandem. One person poses a "What if?" question and before long everyone in the family is wondering, "What if?" "What if I don't get that raise?" "What if we lose our home?" "What if this sickness is really something bigger?" Our worries grow, like yeast-filled rolls. Most of the time the things we're fretting over never come to pass. Whether they do or they don't, worry definitely doesn't add anything positive to the experience. In fact, it takes away from it. So don't worry! Just place your concerns in God's hands. He's got this.

Lord, we've wasted a lot of time worrying about things that never happened. We sure didn't add anything to our lives. Help us in this area. We need to lay down our anxieties and trust You. We choose to do that today, Lord, but we're definitely going to need Your help. Amen.

The righteous cry, and the LORD hears and delivers
them out of all their troubles.
PSALM 34:17 NASB

Have you ever gone to your room, closed the door, and had a long, hard cry? Sometimes we have to do that to get the emotions out. It's not always easy in a household with a lot of other people around, but it's the best way to feel a sense of relief. Did you know that God hears you cry, even when no one else does? He not only sees your tears, He hears the actual cry of your heart—the reason behind the tears. But wait, there's more! When God hears your heart's cry, He springs to action and delivers you out of all of your troubles. Wow! That's an amazing promise, isn't it? So don't be afraid to cry out to God. Not only is He ready to ease your pain, He's already got a solution for your problem.

Lord, we're so glad You hear our cries. We know we can
trust You with our emotions, Father, and we know You
already have an answer for what's troubling us.
Thank You so much for caring enough to wipe away
our tears and move on our behalf. Amen.

Blessed is the one who perseveres under trial because,
having stood the test, that person will
receive the crown of life that the Lord has
promised to those who love him.

JAMES 1:12 NIV

How do you keep going when everything inside of you
tells you to stop? How do you get out of bed in the morning
when you'd rather pull the covers over your head? How do
you go on, day after day, when you've been faced with trial
after trial? There's really only one answer to all of these
questions: perseverance. To *persevere* means you move
forward, even when moving forward seems impossible.
How do you do this? Only by the power of the Spirit. God
can accomplish through you what you could never do for
yourself. And when you persevere, the payoff is amazing!
You will eventually reach the finish line if you don't give
up. So, make up your mind today. Don't quit. Get out of bed.
Put one foot in front of the other. Keep moving, even if it
makes no sense. Persevere.

Father, there are days when we feel like giving up.
We know You've called us to keep going, so that's what
we choose to do. It's hard, Lord. Help us, we pray. Amen.

SHINING YOUR LIGHT

"In the same way, let your good deeds shine out for all to see, so that everyone will praise your heavenly Father."
MATTHEW 5:16 NLT

Some people enjoy being in the spotlight. Others, not so much. In a family environment there are sure to be people of both persuasions. One thing is for sure: When we decide to let the light of Jesus shine through us, we're placing ourselves center stage in front of a watching world. People take notice. How do we shine His light? By loving others. By responding with kindness. By caring for those less fortunate. When we do these things, His light shines bright. We're not doing them to gain attention, not by any stretch, but folks can't help but notice when God's light is shining through us. And when they see it, they are drawn to Him. Before long, their lights are shining bright, too.

We love shining Your light, Father. We're not trying to draw attention to ourselves. We just want others to know of Your great love so that they can share in the joy, too! Thanks for the awesome privilege of living for You. Amen.

He is before all things,
and in him all things hold together.
COLOSSIANS 1:17 NIV

- - - - - - - - - - - - - - - - - - - -

Ever feel like things in your family are coming unglued?
Maybe one fiasco after another hits and there's nothing
you can do about it? If so, then today's verse should
bring great comfort. God is our heavenly glue. He's the
one who holds things together. No matter what you're
facing—as an individual or a family—He's the answer. He's
the glue. In fact, He's been in the fixing business since
the beginning of time. In Him all things hold together:
nations, people, situations. The things you're facing right
now can be fixed with the touch of a fingertip from our
Almighty God. Trust Him. . .and watch Him glue things
back together.

Lord, we're so grateful You're in the fixing business.
There are so many broken areas in our lives, in our family,
in our church. You can fix them all with a whisper, Lord.
Please intervene and have Your way, Father! Amen.

IT'S A RACE!

Therefore, since we are surrounded by such a great cloud of witnesses, let us throw off everything that hinders and the sin that so easily entangles. And let us run with perseverance the race marked out for us, fixing our eyes on Jesus, the pioneer and perfecter of faith.
HEBREWS 12:1–2 NIV

Imagine trying to run a race with a backpack filled with weights strapped to your back. It would slow you down, or, at the very least, cause you pain. Life is a race, and we often try to run with unnecessary weights strapped to us: unforgiveness, guilt, pain, and so on. If we toss those things aside, our pace will be better, our breathing will steady, and we can get to the finish line quicker. God never intended for us to run, run, run with unnecessary baggage. He wants us to give those things to Him so that we will be freed up to soar! So, let's fix our eyes on Him, toss the luggage, and head straight for that finish line!

Lord, we admit, we sometimes try to run with too many weights dragging us down. Today we choose to let go of the things that are holding us captive. We want to run straight to Your arms, Father. . .free and uninhibited. Amen.

"If you love me, obey my commands."
JOHN 14:15 NIrV

It's tempting to read this scripture and quickly move on
to the next one. We don't care much for the idea that love
and obedience go hand in hand, but they do! When a
child loves his parents, he obeys them. The same is true
with us, God's kids. The way we prove our love is to
follow His commands. Which commands? Oh, little
things like: "Do unto others as you would have others do
unto you." That sort of thing. Or maybe, "In all your ways
acknowledge Him." Here's the good part: Obedience
comes naturally to those who love. It's not a sacrifice or an
act of service. It's a true reflection of a loving heart, one
that seeks to please out of a genuine desire to do right by
the other person.

Father, we want to do right by You. We love You so much.
May our acts of obedience come naturally, Lord,
out of a deep, abiding love. Your commands are
never a burden. They are our joy! Amen.

CLEAR THE ROAD!

We put no stumbling block in anyone's path,
so that our ministry will not be discredited.
2 CORINTHIANS 6:3 NIV

Imagine you're in the car, driving down the road. Suddenly, from out of nowhere, there's a car bumper in the road ahead of you. You try to dodge it, but can't do so without hitting a car in the next lane. So you have no choice but to hit it. When you do, it blows out your front tires and sends you veering off the highway onto the shoulder. Stumbling blocks are just like that car bumper. They appear, out of nowhere, and cause serious damage if we don't avoid them. This is why the Lord is so purposeful in telling us that we are not to be a stumbling block for anyone. Everything we do has to help people to their destination, not hurt them. Take a close look at those you're mentoring and make sure the words coming from your mouth are pure and holy, not a stumbling block. Then, tread carefully!

Lord, we don't want to be stumbling blocks. We want our ministry to be effective, not destructive. Help us as we lead others, Father. May we guide them toward You, never injuring them in the process. Amen.

GOD-PLEASERS

Picture a little boy on the ball field. He's pitching his first
game. He throws the ball and it veers off in the wrong
direction. Instead of looking at the ball, the little boy
glances to the stands where his dad sits. Is Dad mad
because he messed up? This might seem like a silly
illustration but we do this all the time. We focus so much
on what others think and it's pointless. We need to remain
focused on what God thinks. When we resort to people-
pleasing we get distracted every time. The Lord longs for
us to please Him, not others. Besides, we'll never win the
approval of men, not for long, anyway. People are fickle,
after all.

*Lord, we know what it feels like to want to make others
happy. We've been seeking approval from others and that's
not necessary or good for us. So today the only thing we're
seeking, Father, is You. And we know that You already
adore us. Bless You for that. Amen.*

HIS STRENGTH

Be strong. Be strong in heart,
all you who hope in the Lord.
PSALM 31:24 NLV

- - - - - - - - - - - - - - - - -

It's so easy for us to use those words, "Be strong" when talking to someone else. They're a little harder to apply to our own situations. When facing a financial challenge, we should tell ourselves, "Be strong!" When going through a relational challenge, we need to repeat those words again: "Be strong!" When everything seems to be tumbling out of control and nothing makes sense, the only words that do are, "Be strong!" And here's the good news: We don't have to summon up strength from out of nowhere. We don't have to pretend to be brave when we're really not. We simply put our trust in God and His strength is made available to us. It's not our strength at all. We are just the vessel through which His power flows. So open your heart and prepare yourself today to be very, very strong.

We're so grateful Your strength flows through us, Lord.
We couldn't summon it up on our own, that's for sure.
Thanks for making us brave, Father. We're facing a lot of
challenges and need all the help we can get. Amen.

See what great love the Father has lavished on us,
that we should be called children of God!
And that is what we are!
1 JOHN 3:1 NIV

God calls us His children. What a sweet Daddy He is! Imagine your family decided to adopt a child, perhaps an older child. He's come from a rough background and never really had a safe home environment. From the minute he comes through the door at your house he's told, "Hey, just call us Mom and Dad. You're our child now." Can you imagine how that would feel to someone who's never had a sense of belonging? To be swept into a family means you get all of the benefits that the others get. They pour their love on you. You belong. You're part of a larger whole. And that's just how it is in God's family. You're one of the gang now. Settle in and prepare to be one of the kids!

Father, we're Your children. Doesn't matter if we're young or old, we're still Your children! Thank You for adopting us and calling us Your own. We have a place to belong now, and we're so grateful. Amen.

Blessed is the people of whom this is true;
blessed is the people whose God is the Lord.
PSALM 144:15 NIV

- - - - - - - - - - - - - - - - - - - -

What does it mean to be blessed? Does it mean that you
receive special favors that others don't? Does it mean
you're the most special kid in the family and that the
others get overlooked? To be blessed simply means
that God pours out all that He has on you. It's like being
a kid on Christmas, only Christmas comes 365 days a
year. The blessings never stop. God doesn't withhold His
blessings. He doesn't say, "I'll give you enough to make
you wish you had more but then I'll stop." He lavishes us.
(All grandparents know what it means to lavish! We just
can't help ourselves!) God's kids are "above and beyond"
blessed by their loving Father, and all for one reason:
Because He loves them.

Lord, it's great to be loved. And we want to pause today to
thank You, specifically, for lavishing Your blessings on us.
We've done nothing to deserve them, but You adore us and
bless us anyway, and we're so grateful! Amen.

MIRROR, MIRROR

*Your beauty should not come from outward adornment,
such as elaborate hairstyles and the wearing of gold
jewelry or fine clothes. Rather, it should be that of your
inner self, the unfading beauty of a gentle and quiet spirit,
which is of great worth in God's sight.*

1 PETER 3:3–4 NIV

Most of us have a love-hate relationship with the mirror.
On the days the reflection in the mirror looks good to
us, we love it. On the days we don't care for the way we
look, we hate it. It's time to look beyond the image in the
mirror to what really matters—the person inside. Beauty
goes much deeper than what you can see with your eyes.
A truly beautiful person has a gentle and quiet spirit. No
amount of makeup or jewelry can make a bitter, hurtful
person beautiful, and no amount of physical flaws on the
outside can make a loving, gentle person ugly. Beauty. It's
what's on the inside that counts.

*Lord, we're grateful for the reminder that we need to be
beautiful from the inside out. When others see us,
may they see Your love shining through. Amen.*

"Be strong and very courageous. Be careful to obey all the law my servant Moses gave you; do not turn from it to the right or to the left, that you may be successful wherever you go."

JOSHUA 1: 7–9 NIV

- - - - - - - - - - - - - - - - - -

The words of the Bible are God's holy guidelines for us to live by. When we choose to both read and obey, we're placing ourselves within the confines of the Word. Those confines aren't meant to restrict us; in fact, they're meant to free us! When we make up our minds not to veer to the right or left (not to take the words of the Bible and twist them to suit our way of thinking) we're really being freed up to live in God's fullness. Why is the Lord so keen on seeing us live by His precepts? Because, with them comes success! In fact, today's scripture teaches us that choosing to walk a biblical path will cause us to be successful wherever we go. What a wonderful blessing!

Lord, for the sake of our family and our own lives, keep us walking the straight and narrow, we pray. Amen.

Don't let anyone look down on you because you are young,
but set an example for the believers in speech,
in conduct, in love, in faith and in purity.
1 TIMOTHY 4:12 NIV

God is not a respecter of persons. He doesn't value one human life above another. And He doesn't limit us by age either. In fact, today's verse is proof that the Lord finds great value in young people. He feels so strongly about them, in fact, that He encourages them to hold their heads up high and set an example for others by the way they live. How is this example set? In speech (the way words are used to lift others up or tear them down). In love (sharing God's love with all, even the most unloveable). In faith (trust in God in impossible situations). In purity (choosing to remain pure in thought and deed). In all these ways a young person can lead by example. And others who follow can carry on for generations to come.

Lord, we're so glad You don't want anyone to look down on
young people. You're not a respecter of persons.
Everyone has value, and everyone can lead by example.
Thank You for trusting Your kids with
such a mighty task. Amen.

COURTESY

To speak evil of no one, to avoid quarreling, to be gentle,
and to show perfect courtesy toward all people.
TITUS 3:2 ESV

Common courtesy. We don't hear those words much
anymore, do we? *Common* means you do it without being
asked to. It just comes naturally. *Courtesy* is treating
others with the respect they deserve, not because of any
special position they hold, but simply because they're
part of the family. They're God's kids. So, what will it take
to lay down quarreling in your household? First, it has to
be acknowledged and then dealt with. If the days slip by
and no one admits to the problem it will only get worse.
When quarreling and strife end, gentleness takes over.
Then, when the waters are calm, there's room for sensible
thinking. Where there is sensible thinking, courtesy
follows. So, acknowledge the need for peace in the
household and watch these other things fall into place.

Lord, we admit we sometimes bicker. In fact, the quarreling
gets out of hand sometimes and not just between the kids.
Show us how to get past this in our family, we pray,
and then guide us all to a place of common courtesy,
where all are respected, regardless of age. Amen.

*"Now then, my children, listen to me; blessed are those
who keep my ways. Listen to my instruction
and be wise; do not disregard it."*
PROVERBS 8:32–33 NIV

- -

It's hard to listen to instructions. Don't believe it? Think
about the last time you were on an airplane and the flight
attendant started the routine flight safety speech. You
probably zoned out. There's something about listening
to the rules that causes us to check out. But we can't do
that where God's Word is concerned. He's got specific
instructions for us, and they're life changing. Like the
instructions that flight attendant is giving us, they could
save our life. When we take the time to not only listen
to but apply the Lord's rules, we obtain wisdom. We're
blessed when we keep His ways. So, when the Lord
speaks, listen up! His plans for you are higher. In fact, like
that airplane flight—they're out of this world.

*Lord, we'll be the first to admit we're not big fans of
rules and regulations. But when You speak, Father,
we'll listen. We don't want to miss Your instruction because
we know it's life-giving. So we're all ears, Lord. Amen.*

JEALOUSY, BE GONE!

But if you have bitter jealousy and selfish ambition in your hearts, do not boast and be false to the truth.
JAMES 3:14 ESV

Jealousy rears its head when we least expect it, often catching us off guard. It shows up in children, teens, and adults. It always uses the same words, "What about me?" It always points to self instead of others. It's always rooted in pain and insecurity. It often leads to broken relationships and bitterness. Sometimes that bitterness can drag on for years. It's better to recognize jealousy and selfish ambition at the onset of a situation and deal with it immediately. Ask God to remove the blinders from your eyes so that you can see clearly. Then admit your jealousies and ask Him to rid your heart of them. When you're free from jealousy, it changes everything—your actions, your attitudes, and your outcome. It also puts your focus where it belongs, on God and on building others up instead of tearing them down.

Lord, we've been guilty of jealousy. It's gotten in the way of some of our relationships. Thank You for removing it from our hearts. We're grateful to walk in freedom, Lord! Amen.

Suppose a brother or sister is without clothes and daily food. If one of you says to them, "Go, in peace; keep warm and well fed," but does nothing about their physical needs, what good is it? In the same way, faith by itself, if it is not accompanied by action, is dead.

JAMES 2:15–17 NIV

We're always using the phrase, "family first." It is important to make sure our family members are well cared for. Fed. Clothed. Have a room over their heads. But there's a larger family out there, one we're also told to look after. All around us there are people who are hurting. They're homeless. Out of work. Abused. Lonely. Hungry. In need of basic necessities. We're not able to care for all of their needs, but what if we took on one simple task—say, providing a meal to an elderly couple once a week? Wouldn't that make a difference to that couple? There's always something we can do. And we're still putting "family first" as long as we're tending to the people in God's family.

Lord, we get it! Family first! Your family surrounds us on every side. Show us how we can best minister to Your family, Father. We want to share Your love with as many as we can. Amen.

GOD'S MEDICINE. . .A JOYFUL HEART

A joyful heart is good medicine,
but a broken spirit dries up the bones.
PROVERBS 17:22 NASB

We all know what it's like to have a bad cold. We're congested. Coughing. Feverish. Shivering under the blankets, we pray that it will pass. . .quickly. Just about the time we're ready to give up, medicine arrives. An hour later, we're already feeling its effects. We're less stuffy. Our fever is dropping. Even the cough has lessened. Medicine, when used at the right time, can change everything. Isn't it interesting that the Bible calls a joyful heart good medicine? And it's a medicine we always have on hand. We simply have to remind ourselves, in the middle of the icky situations, that it's right there, waiting to be used. When our hearts spring to life, our broken spirits and our spiritual health are restored. What a lovely medicine!

We're grateful for this reminder that a happy, joyful heart
is good medicine, Lord. It's not always easy to be joyful,
but it's just what You've called us to do. Today we choose
joy. We know that our situation will be eased once
we swallow this godly medicine. Amen.

NO BUSYBODIES!

*For we hear that some among you are leading an
undisciplined life, doing no work at all,
but acting like busybodies.*
2 THESSALONIANS 3:11 NASB

Have you ever contemplated the word *busybody*? It's
a common word to describe a body (person) who's in
someone else's business! God never intended for us to
be busybodies. In fact, our own lives have enough drama
without borrowing from our neighbors. So why put our
noses in where they don't belong? We don't need to tell
others how to live, how to be better Christians, when
we haven't even made progress in that area ourselves.
Better to discipline ourselves, mind our own business, let
God take the reins of our lives, and then let Him do the
same with our neighbors. The Lord is a far better teacher,
anyway. He has a way of winning people over without any
hard feelings or gossip at all.

*Lord, we don't want to be busybodies. We ask for Your
forgiveness, Lord, and Your grace. Thank You
for Your mercy. Amen.*

It is for freedom that Christ has set us free.
Stand firm, then, and do not let yourselves
be burdened again by a yoke of slavery.
GALATIANS 5:1 NIV

Imagine a slave who's given his life in service to his master. He's done everything he's been told to do. He's taken abuse at the hands of his overseer and borne it without flinching. Finally someone purchases his freedom. Only, now he's confused. The shackles are gone, but now what? Who will provide his meals? What does he do with himself, now that he's not obligated to his former owner? So, he opts to go back to his evil master, convinced it's the only life for him. Perhaps this analogy seems extreme, but that's often how we live. Christ sets us free from the curse of the law and we end up returning to our former lives, convinced we had it better back then. Christ has set us free to remain free! We must stand firm and not allow the yoke of slavery to take hold of us, ever again.

Father, we want to remain free! We don't want to go back
to our old lives. We felt captured, bound. Help us to
stand firm, Lord. We refuse that yoke of slavery.
We cast it off, in Jesus' name! Amen.

WHAT SEASON ARE YOU IN?

There is a time for everything, and a season for
every activity under the heavens.
ECCLESIASTES 3:1 NIV

We all walk though seasons in our lives. Some are happier
than others. Some are more productive than others.
Some are quieter, more restful than others. No matter
the season your family is in, don't fight it. Just remember
that all seasons come to an end. Winter shifts to spring,
spring to summer, and so on. When you fight the seasons,
you wear yourself out, and all to no avail. Time will pass.
Seasons will change. Whatever challenges you're walking
through at this very moment will be nothing but a distant
memory someday. Until then, look up! Keep your focus
on God and trust that He will see you through until the
winds change.

Lord, we're glad this is only a season. We're not sure we
could handle it if the circumstances in our lives stayed
the same forever. Thank You for shifting winds, Father.
We can hear them blowing, and we look forward to
whatever is coming next. Until then,
we choose to trust You. Amen.

> *"You did not choose me, but I chose you and appointed*
> *you so that you might go and bear fruit—fruit that will*
> *last—and so that whatever you ask in my name*
> *the Father will give you."*
> JOHN 15:16 NIV

Picture yourself at the supermarket, hovering over a bin of apples. You've made up your mind to choose six of them to purchase, but which six? You look them over, examining them for bruises and soft spots. Finally you decide on one. It's not perfect, but you're sure it's just right for you. Then you find another. And another. When we have the option of "choosing" we're careful with what we select. Imagine how God must feel! He had the option of choosing us. In fact, He not only chose us, He appointed us as well. To do what, you ask? To bear fruit of course. You were chosen specifically by God because He knew you would bear fruit in your life. And fruit bearers are capable of changing the world.

Lord, we're so honored that You chose us—You saw
our potential. We're so honored. May we bear fruit
for You, Father. We want to bless You for
putting Your trust in us. Amen.

From the end of the earth I will cry to You,
when my heart is overwhelmed; lead me to
the rock that is higher than I.
PSALM 61:2 NKJV

Everyone knows that "overwhelmed" feeling. It hits us on a near-continual basis. Things are spinning so fast around us that it's hard to focus sometimes. Family obligations. Bills. School. Relationships. Church obligations. Illness. Unexpected crises. These things always seem to catch us off guard. When we're overwhelmed, we have that "drowning" sensation. God never intended for us to live like that. He's the buoy we need to lift us up when we're down. Only He can take away that feeling of being overwhelmed and replace it with peace. So, when our hearts are heavy, we have to cry out to Him. He is truly the rock that is higher, higher, higher, far above the circumstances that threaten to bring us down.

Oh Father, sometimes we feel so overwhelmed.
There's so much busy-ness around us.
But You, Lord, can manage it all.
Please remind us that we can come to You
when we're overwhelmed. Amen.

SATISFIED IN HIM

Satisfy us in the morning with your unfailing love,
that we may sing for joy and be glad all our days.
PSALM 90:14 NIV

Has anyone ever loved you unconditionally? Has anyone ever said, "No matter how many times you fall down, I'll always pick you up again?" Only the Lord can promise to love with no conditions attached whatsoever. And He genuinely means it when He promises to stick with you through thick and thin. His love is supernatural—above and beyond the realm of the natural. This kind of love, the "unfailing" kind, is enough to keep us satisfied from morning till night. When we grab hold of the fact that we're loved no matter what, it changes us. It makes us want to do better! And it keeps our focus on God. We're completely satisfied in Him because we sense His love, His forgiveness, and His great mercy. What a wonderful way to live!

Father, Your unconditional love is beyond anything
we've ever experienced. We're so grateful. Others would've
turned and run the opposite direction by now, but You,
Lord. . .You stick with us. You bless us even when
we don't deserve it. Amen.

You should not stay away from the church meetings,
as some are doing, but you should meet together
and encourage each other. Do this even more
as you see the day coming.
HEBREWS 10:25 NCV

What a blessing the church is, not just for individuals, but whole families. The church is the ideal place to settle in, to gain friendships, to grow in faith. When we stay away, we have a tendency to feel like outsiders, and this only makes us want to stay away even more. So, dig your heels in. Get involved. Get connected. Become vulnerable. Let people love on you, and vice-versa. Allow yourself the joy—and sometimes the pain—of being in relationship with others in the body of Christ. When others peek inside the doors and see people living in harmony, they are drawn in. That's a lovely thing.

Father, thank You for our church. We're grateful to be
surrounded by people who love You and love us. I pray that
our family would settle in for the long haul,
ready to work alongside brothers and sisters in Christ as
the Gospel goes forth. Amen.

*He gives strength to the weary and increases the power
of the weak. Even youths grow tired and weary,
and young men stumble and fall; but those who hope
in the LORD will renew their strength.*
ISAIAH 40:29-30 NIV

- -

There are some days when we wish we could just stay
in bed all day. We're tired to the bone, as the old saying
goes. But we drag ourselves out of bed determined to turn
things around. Most of the time we still drag through the
day, unable to give it our best. There's nothing shameful
in being tired. The Bible says that even the youths grow
tired and weary. It's not just an age thing. But what do we
do about it? We have to keep going, after all. The very
best thing we can do when we're worn out is to pray for
supernatural strength. God will surely energize you with
His strength and His power. Then, when the timing's right,
we need to rest. It's a necessary part of the equation.

*Lord, we get so tired. The exhaustion overwhelms us at
times. We wonder if we can go on. When we reach that
point, Father, please energize us. We know You'll do it,
Lord, and we're grateful. Amen.*

LIFT UP YOUR HEAD

But You, O Lord, are a shield for me,
my glory and the One who lifts up my head.
PSALM 3:3 NKJV

- -

Have you ever felt so weighted down that your head literally felt heavy? When you're going through a "heavy" season, keeping your focus on God can be tough. And when your whole family is going through a heavy season, it can be even harder, because the weight of so many people being down at the same time seems impossible to overcome. Oh, but we serve a God who wants us to supernaturally live weightless lives! He wants to lift our eyes to Him because He's the great weight lifter. Instead of carrying around all of the burdens ourselves, we can shift our focus and transfer the heaviness to His shoulders. He can handle it. We cannot. So lift those eyes. Look to Him. Then watch as the weight of the situation eases and you're light as a feather once more.

Father, sometimes we feel so weighted down. We can't imagine passing off our burdens to You. But You long for us to do this, Lord, and we want to try. Please take these weights and carry them for us. We lift our heads and our eyes to You, Lord! Amen.

But godliness with contentment is great gain.
1 TIMOTHY 6:6 KJV

- -

Contentment. It's one of those things we talk about but don't always have. It's hard to be content when we're always longing for more, isn't it? And yet, that's just what God calls us to do. When we're content in Him, we have the whole world at our feet. When we live in discontentment, always wishing we had something more, something different, we're so hyper-focused on that, that we miss the good things. What are you struggling with today? What area of your life provides the most opportunity for discontentment? Instead of griping and complaining, begin to praise God. Even if there's a lack, praise Him for the things you do have. Then watch as discontentment turns to peace, contentment, and even joy.

Father, please take our discontentment. We lay it at Your feet, Lord. It's messing up our thoughts and making us envious of others. Show us how to live a contented life, filled with praise for all You've done. We choose to start today by praising You, Lord! You are worthy of all our praise. Amen.

"This book of the Law must not leave your mouth. Think about it day and night, so you may be careful to do all that is written in it. Then all will go well with you. You will receive many good things."
JOSHUA 1:8 NLV

Here's a fun idea for your family: Start a scripture memorization plan. Choose a scripture a week for everyone in the family to memorize. Write it on a slip of paper and put it where it can be seen: on the refrigerator door, the inside of your front door, even on the bathroom mirror. Another great idea is to set it to melody. Turn it into a song which is easier to remember, and you can even sing it together. Memorized scriptures come to mind whenever we're in a jam. We won't even have to think about it. When we're facing an obstacle, the perfect scripture will come to mind. That's the joy of thinking about the Word day and night.

Lord, please help us memorize strategic verses so that they will be fresh on our minds when we need them. We love the promise that dwelling on Your Word will cause things to go well with us. What a blessing, Father! Amen.

I'M SO OFFENDED!

Good sense makes one slow to anger,
and it is his glory to overlook an offense.
PROVERBS 19:11 ESV

Have you ever thought about the difference between the two words *defend* and *offend*? When you're on the defense, you're prepared for anything that comes your way. Unfortunately, many of us choose the "offend" side instead of the "defend" side. We get our feelings hurt, sometimes too easily. Instead of being prepared for these instances, we are caught off guard. We curl up in a ball, wounded. It's time to join the defense! Prepare yourself—prepare your family—for attacks. They will come. And when they do, you will stand strong, ready to meet them. You won't cower, offended and hurt. You will hold up your head, stronger than ever, and recognize the attack for what it is. . .a ploy from the enemy.

Sometimes we get offended, Lord. It's hard not to!
We're glad You've reminded us that we need to be on the
defense. Today we choose not to be offended. We choose
to lift our heads and our hearts, ready for anything the
enemy might toss our way. With You, Lord,
we are stronger than any foe. Amen.

*"Truly I tell you, if anyone says to this mountain,
'Go, throw yourself into the sea,' and does not doubt
in their heart but believes that what they say
will happen, it will be done for them."*
MARK 11:23 NIV

- - - - - - - - - - - - - - - - - - - -

Mountain moving sounds like excruciating work! The truth is, mountain moving isn't a matter of physical labor. The Bible said we can speak to the mountains (obstacles) in our lives and they will disappear like a puff of smoke. We can say, "Go, throw yourself into the sea!" and those obstacles have to disappear. The next time your family is facing a mountain, instead of trying to figure out how you can all work together to move it, try linking arms, facing it, and speaking directly to it. Then watch as it tumbles into the sea.

*Lord, our family has faced a lot of mountains.
They seem insurmountable. But we delight in the
impossible, so today we choose to speak to the mountains.
In faith, we will watch them disappear!
Thank You for the courage to believe
for the impossible, Lord. Amen.*

Don't let the excitement of youth cause you to forget your Creator. Honor him in your youth before you grow old and say, "Life is not pleasant anymore."
ECCLESIASTES 12:1 NLT

We're only young once. How many times we've heard that phrase! Many people take this to mean they should go for the gusto in their youth, live life to the fullest, throw caution to the wind. They are so interested in partying and having a blast that they sometimes forget all about the call of God on their lives. While it's true that God wants us to live fulfilled (fun, happy) lives, He cares far more about having us stick close to Him. So, remember to put God first, no matter your age. You don't want to reach the point where you've drifted so far away from Him that you say, "What happened to my life? Nothing's any good anymore." Stick close. He will still give you the ride of your life, and you'll come out closer to Him than ever.

Father, we want to stick close. Sure, we want to have a good time, too, but with You leading and guiding, we can. You aren't trying to ruin our fun, Lord. We can trust You to still give us an awesome ride, one that takes us to a happily-ever-after. Amen.

You also, like living stones, are being built into a spiritual house to be a holy priesthood, offering spiritual sacrifices acceptable to God through Jesus Christ.
1 PETER 2:5 NIV

We're called to be a holy house. Not a house made of brick and stone, of course, but a spiritual house, with an amazing foundation and lovely interior. How do we accomplish this? By working hard? By putting our best foot forward and investing in landscaping help? Nope. We start with the foundational core of having a solid relationship with Jesus. We offer our lives as a sacrifice and let Him take up residence inside of us. A house that's filled with God is a beautiful home, for sure! When others look at us, may they see beyond the exterior (our looks, our shape, our flaws) and see straight to the heart. . .His heart. And when they look at our family, may the light of the Lord come shining through.

Lord, we want to be a beautiful house, not just externally but internally. We want Your light to shine out of the windows of our eyes so that people will be drawn to us, and ultimately to You. Thank You for placing Your Spirit inside of us, Lord. What a privilege, this holy priesthood! Amen.

KNOWN BY YOUR ACTIONS

Even small children are known by their actions,
so is their conduct really pure and upright?
PROVERBS 20:11 NIV

Picture the poor school teacher with a roomful of little ones. Some are well behaved; others, not so much. She does her best to treat them all the same, but a couple of them give her a run for her money. The truth is, we're known by our actions, good or bad. They establish our reputation. This might seem innocent enough when we're talking about little kids, but big kids are known for their actions as well. When our conduct is pure and right, we win the confidence of those around us. When we're always lashing out, hurting others, and demanding we get our own way, it's a huge turn off. May we, as individuals, be known for our good actions. And may our family be respected because we've chosen to honor God in everything we do.

Father, what a reminder! Our actions speak so much
louder than our words. We can say all day long that we
love people, but if our actions speak otherwise, then we're
being hypocrites. Help us today, Lord. We want to be
known as ones who are loving and trustworthy. Amen.

NEVER FORSAKEN

"Never will I leave you; never will I forsake you."
HEBREWS 13:5 NIV

- -

If you've ever struggled with feelings of abandonment or betrayal, you might have trouble believing that God will never leave you or forsake you. This is especially true if you're in the middle of walking through a breakup in a relationship. No matter what you're facing in the natural, God's Word is true. You can take it to the bank. He's not leaving. There's nothing you've done, nothing you'll ever do, that could possibly drive Him away. He's sticking to you like glue. You might as well get used to the idea. No abandonment here. God's going all the way with you, in good times and in bad. He also wants to heal you of the pain you might be feeling as a result of someone else's rejection. Hang on to Him today. Receive the hope and healing you need to move forward, confident in the fact that He's with you, every step of the way.

We needed this reminder today, Lord. You're with us. You're not forsaking us. We ask You to heal our hearts. We've been wounded in the past, but we want to move forward. With Your help, we can, Father. Thank You for giving us hope again. Amen.

A KIND WORD

*Anxiety weighs down the heart,
but a kind word cheers it up.*
PROVERBS 12:25 NIV

- -

Have you ever been really, really down? So low that you wanted to crawl in bed and pull the covers over your head? That's what anxiety will do to you! This can be greatly exaggerated in a family situation because people tend to drag others down when they're feeling low. When someone in the family begins this process, speak life and joy over the situation. Speak hope and healing. Hope can go a long, long way in diffusing anxiety. Commit scriptures to memory and speak them aloud. Do your best to have a positive word, even when others around you are negative. Your positivity can turn their negativity around in a hurry. Or, at the very least, it can keep your heart and mind focused on God.

Lord, we know how anxiety pulls people down. We've all been in that spot many times. We want to be the ones sharing hope. Joy. A positive word. Give us the courage, in the moment, to speak up and offer kind words instead of joining in the groveling. We'll need Your help, Father, but we know You're quick to give it. Amen.

LEGACY LEAVERS

The word of the LORD came to me, saying, "Before I formed you in the womb I knew you, before you were born I set you apart; I appointed you as a prophet to the nations."
JEREMIAH 1:4–5 NIV

- - - - - - - - - - - - - - - - - - - -

We all want to be legacy leavers, people who keep our godly heritage going from generation to generation. This is especially true in the family environment where we have the opportunity to pass on biblical truths to our children and grandchildren (and so on). God has appointed us as prophets to the nations and our "nations" begin at home. We've been set apart to accomplish great things for Him. No matter what else we leave behind (our belongings, our name, our home) the most important thing by far is a passion for Christ. May all of our descendants carry on the legacy of loving God and putting Him first!

You've called us and set us apart, Lord. We're so grateful. The "nation" we're called to reach starts inside our own home. Thank You for that reminder. In faith we will claim that our family members will all be legacy leavers, impacting the world for the sake of the Gospel. What a privilege, Father. Bless You for that. Amen.

GOD WILL WORK IT FOR OUR GOOD

And we know that in all things God works for the good
of those who love him, who have been called
according to his purpose.
ROMANS 8:28 NIV

- -

Do we really trust God to turn the bad things in our lives
for good? It's easy to say, "Why, sure!" but do we really
mean it? Can we prove it with our actions when things
aren't going our way? Many times we're in the throes of
the battle and can't see past the fog. It's hard to trust that
better days are coming. But even then God promises to
work it out for good. May our hearts be settled, even in
the storm. May they remain calm, even when arrows are
flying around us. May they be ever-faithful, convinced
that God's greater purpose will be fulfilled.

We want to believe it, Lord! We want to believe that
everything will work together for our good as long as
we place our love and trust in You. Today we choose to
do that, Father. Things don't always make sense, but we
choose to trust. I'm confident You are working on our
behalf and the outcome will be good. Amen.

Above all else, guard your heart,
for everything you do flows from it.
PROVERBS 4:23 NIV

What does it mean to have a guarded heart? To place
a guard around your heart means you don't knee-jerk
when offended or hurt. This is especially important in
a family environment, where the potential for flare-ups
is everywhere. When we live in a home with others, the
temptation to snap is greater than usual because we're so
close—physically, emotionally, and otherwise. But taking
a breath, taking a step back, is always the best route. A
guarded heart is a safe heart. A happy heart. A peaceful
heart. A guarded heart looks out for others instead of self.
Now that's a fine way to live!

Lord, we needed this reminder. Sometimes we knee-jerk.
We don't guard our hearts. Today we ask that You
intervene and teach us how to take a deep breath
and think before we act. Guard our hearts, Father.
We place them in Your loving hands. Amen.

WONDERFULLY MADE

For you created my inmost being; you knit me together
in my mother's womb. I praise you because I am
fearfully and wonderfully made; your works are
wonderful, I know that full well.
PSALM 139:13–14 NIV

- -

What an artist our heavenly Father is! He's a knitter, a
crafter, a true artiste! His paintings aren't hanging in a
museum; they are on display all around us—in a colorful
sunset, a child's sweet face. And we're part of His great
design. Our bodies—no matter the shape or size—were
knit together in our mother's womb, specifically designed
by the greatest artist of all time. We are fearfully and
wonderfully made. He took great care when creating
us. God's works are wonderful. It's time we embraced
that reality and began to thank Him for creating us with
such intricate detail. Our very creative God is a master
designer. No doubt about it.

Father, we're so grateful for Your design! Your blueprint
for our bodies, our minds, and our hearts were—and are—
perfect. You thoughtfully knit us together in our mothers'
wombs, and Your works—each one of us!—are wonderful.
Thank You for that reminder today, Lord. Amen.

HE WON'T WITHHOLD

*For the L*ORD *God is a sun and shield; the L*ORD *bestows
favor and honor; no good thing does he withhold from
those whose walk is blameless.*

PSALM 84:11 NIV

- - - - - - - - - - - - - - - - - - -

Picture yourself going to the grocery store and buying a
bag of your favorite candy. You take it home and hide it
in a cabinet, way up high where no one will ever discover
it. Sneaking pieces of candy becomes an art form, as you
try to keep your goodies to yourself. Aren't you glad God
doesn't employ this method? He doesn't stash gifts on
the top shelf, hoping you won't discover them. All of his
goodies are within reach. Not only that, He wants to share
them with you, even longs to share them with you. Why?
Because He's a generous Father, not stingy. He also knows
that He can use those gifts to draw others to Him, so it's a
win-win situation when He lavishes them on you. What a
generous God we serve!

*Oh Lord, thank You! We needed this reminder that You're
a generous God, ready to bestow favor and honor.
Your many gifts are right in front of us for the taking.
We're so blessed, Lord! Amen.*

A STRAIGHT PATH

*Trust in the L<small>ORD</small> with all your heart and lean not
on your own understanding; in all your ways submit
to him, and he will make your paths straight.*
P<small>ROVERBS</small> 3:5–6 <small>NIV</small>

Picture yourself on a winding trail in the middle of a
state park. You're doing all right, following the well-marked
path, and then. . .*bam*. The road ahead gets fuzzy. It's a
little unclear. Do you go straight or veer off a bit to the
left? You can't really tell; you stop dead in your tracks.
You look around for clues but there are few to be found.
No GPS can help you because the path is rarely traveled.
Sometimes life feels a bit like that, especially in a family
environment. You're going along just fine. You think
you've got a handle on things. Then. . .*bam*. Something
happens and you're not as sure as you were yesterday.
The path isn't clearly marked. On those days, when you're
tempted to stop in your tracks, there's One you can call
out to who knows whether you should veer to the right
or left. Call out to Him and then listen. Closely. He will
guide you, even if it's one baby step at a time.

*Father, we feel so lost sometimes. Thank You for making
things clear when we're feeling lost, Lord. Amen.*

*Now to him who is able to do immeasurably more than all
we ask or imagine, according to his power that is at work
within us, to him be glory in the church and in Christ Jesus
throughout all generations, for ever and ever!*
EPHESIANS 3:20–21 NIV

Picture a shelf in your pantry where you keep things that
you don't want the kids to get into. It's above their reach.
It's so high, so lofty, it's unattainable to them. That's
how God's works are in our lives. If they were attainable,
we could all do them. Nothing would be unreachable
for us. But they're high. They're lofty. They're so far
above anything we could ask or think that we can't help
but marvel. What a magnificent God! How He proves
Himself, time and time again. The next time you're
feeling like there's no way out of a situation, look up! Look
above! Look beyond! He's already working on your behalf,
in ways that will simply take your breath away.

*Oh Lord, may we never forget that Your ways are higher!
The things You're doing for us are light-years beyond
anything we could dream up for ourselves. Thank You for
shifting our focus up, up, up. . .and away from ourselves.
You're truly awesome, Father! Amen.*

GOSSIP

*Whoever covers an offense seeks love, but he who
repeats a matter separates close friends.*
PROVERBS 17:9 ESV

Gossip often starts small, like a little match, lit to a tiny
flame. Before long, it's a raging wildfire, burning down
relationships and leaving a path of destruction behind.
This is especially true in a family environment. One
person says something about another. That story gets
spread to the next person, who makes an assumption that
it's 100 percent true. From there it travels at the speed
of light, growing, morphing, and becoming something
far beyond the original tale. By the time the fire truck
arrives to put it out, the damage has already been done.
Today, before you share a "tiny" story with a friend or
family member, pray about it first. Ask the Lord if the
story is something that should be spread, or something
you should keep to yourself. Many relationships could be
saved, if the match was never lit.

*Father, we ask You to guard our tongues in the moment.
The next time we're tempted, Father, remind us of the
raging fire we're starting, then help us squelch
it before it even begins. Amen.*

Then the cloud covered the meeting tent.
The shining-greatness of the Lord filled the holy tent.
EXODUS 40:34 NLV

- - - - - - - - - - - - - - -

Oh, the glory of the Lord's presence! It's not just
something we read about in the Old Testament. It's
not just Isaiah standing in the temple or Moses on the
mountain. The presence of God is with us every day.
Sometimes we miss it because we're not paying attention.
His holiness, His majesty surrounds us! We witness His
presence in the ocean waves. We breathe it in in the clear
mountain air. We're captivated by it in a baby's smile.
Everywhere we turn, the presence of the Lord greets us.
May we, as a family, recognize it for what it is and give
thanks. May we never be so busy that we overlook the
more brilliant gift of all, God's holy presence.

Father, we've witnessed Your presence so many times.
Your holiness has taken our breath away! You've caused us
to gasp at the splendor of a sunset or the perfect arch of
a brightly colored rainbow. What a magnificent Creator
You are. Thank You, Lord, for inviting us into Your
presence each day. Amen.

"Come now, let us settle the matter," says the LORD.
"Though your sins are like scarlet, they shall be
as white as snow; though they are red as crimson,
they shall be like wool."
ISAIAH 1:18 NIV

Families have a lot of laundry. Sometimes the pile is never-ending! In some ways, our sins are like those dirty, stained pieces of laundry. We mess up so badly we feel there's simply no way to repair the situation. To mend the relationship. To begin again. To make right what we got wrong. Oh, but we serve a God who's in the forgiving business. He can take our stains, our sins, and toss them in His miraculous washer and give them a spin until they're as white as snow. Not even a remnant remains. No trace of what was there before. What an amazing God! How blessed we are to be given a fresh start!

Lord, we're so grateful that You've washed our sins away.
The very things we're most ashamed of are the things we
no longer have to worry about. You've removed every
stain. We can't thank You enough, Father! Amen.

*For God has not given us a spirit of timidity,
but of power and love and discipline.*
2 TIMOTHY 1:7 NASB

Discipline is one thing. Self-discipline, another entirely.
We don't care for discipline when it comes from others
(usually, anyway) but when we have to dish it out on
ourselves it's even tougher to take. Still, this is a necessary
part of life. We have to discipline the body, the mind, and
the heart. If we don't, we'll have no boundaries, no sense
of control. So gear up! No timidity here. Put on power.
Put on love. Put on self-discipline. Then watch as you
grow in your faith and in your convictions. Before long
you'll be able to say no to the things you should reject and
yes to the things you should embrace. Self-discipline is a
necessary part of the equation.

*Father, we don't care much for discipline. We guess You
already know that. You've certainly had to discipline us
a lot over the years. Thank You for teaching us how
to discipline ourselves—our bodies, our hearts,
and our minds. We'll be better off for it, Lord! Amen.*

He maketh me to lie down in green pastures:
he leadeth me beside the still waters.
PSALM 23:2 KJV

Ah, rest! How we love it. How we *need* it. These days, we have so little of it. We're busy, running from place to place, event to event. Rest is such an important part of our walk with the Lord because we don't operate at our best when we're exhausted. There truly are some seasons where God actually leads us beside still waters so that we can take a breather. Picture yourself there now. Green pastures. A quiet stream in the distance. Gently flowing waters. A weeping willow tree overhead. The sound of crickets in the background. What a lovely image, and what a precious place to meet with God. He desires nothing more than for us to quiet our hearts so that they are open to hear what He wants to speak to us. May we be attentive and ready.

Lord, we want to hear Your voice. Draw us to still waters
today, we pray. Drown out the voices of chaos around
us so that we only hear Your heartbeat. May our
hearts beat with Yours, Father. Amen.

FREE FROM FEAR

You will not fear the terror of night,
nor the arrow that flies by day
PSALM 91:5 NIV

There's something about the nighttime that makes us fearful. Perhaps, once the lights go out, we fear the things we can't see. We imagine things that aren't there. God doesn't want us to be afraid though. He's bigger than even our wildest imagination, and He's promised to take care of us, day or night. So, if those arrows fly at you in the daytime, or you lie huddled under the covers at night, fearing every little sound you hear in the house, just know that God is bigger. And when He shows up, every bit of fear has to flee in Jesus' name. So, be brave. Speak to those fears and see them gone in His name.

Lord, we know we can trust You, even when things
go bump in the night. You're such a good God and You
take care of us, in the dark or in the light. Please show us
how to let go of lingering fears so that we're free to
be all You've created us to be. Amen.

RESPECT

*Never speak harshly to an older man, but appeal to him
respectfully as you would to your own father.
Talk to younger men as you would to your own brothers.
Treat older women as you would your mother, and treat younger
women with all purity as you would your own sisters.*

1 TIMOTHY 5:1–2 NLT

Sometimes we look back at how people behaved in
"the olden days" and wonder what the modern world is
coming to. Back then, children were taught to respect
their elders. These days, it seems like disrespect is a way
of life, and not just for young people. Spouses treat each
other disrespectfully. Friends don't respect one another's
feelings. Siblings don't respect boundaries. Why? Because
people are so busy looking out for number one. This flies
in the face of God's Word. When we live the Lord's way,
we treat others the way we would want to be treated. Our
words should be laced with love. Might sound difficult,
but definitely not impossible. With His help, all things
are possible.

*Father, please show us what it means to treat others
with respect. We want our family to learn the art of
respectfulness so that we can glorify You. Amen!*

For he has rescued us from the dominion of darkness and brought us into the kingdom of the Son he loves, in whom we have redemption, the forgiveness of sins.
COLOSSIANS 1:13–14 NIV

If you've ever traveled on a cruise and stayed in an interior room, you know what total darkness looks like. Without the benefit of a window or balcony door, you can turn off the lights and the whole place shifts to total darkness. That's what living apart from God is like. It's like flipping a switch and not being able to see a thing. Oh, but when Christ comes into our hearts, when the light comes on, we are staggered by the things we see. We've been brought from a place where we had no sense of direction to a place where everything is crystal clear. Praise the Lord for the light! He has rescued us forever from the dark, dreary places and given us a clear path to follow, as individuals and family members.

Lord, we didn't realize how dark our lives were until You drew us into the light. Our eyes are still adjusting at times, Lord, but with Your help we'll see more clearly with each passing day. Praise You, Father! Amen.

CALLED ACCORDING TO HIS PURPOSE

And we know that God causes everything to work together
for the good of those who love God and are called
according to his purpose for them.
ROMANS 8:28 NLT

- - - - - - - - - - - - - - - - - - -

Remember that feeling you had as a kid when your mom
stuck her head out the door and hollered, "Suppertime!"
Her words were a direct call, an invitation to join the
family around the table. You would drop whatever game
you were playing with your friends and go tearing inside,
all because of her call. It's the same when we experience
the call of God in our lives. His voice rings out, bidding
us to come inside, to spend time around the table, and
we feel a sense of joy as we sprint in His direction. When
we run to Him—in good times and bad—He causes
everything we're going through to work together for
good. Our job? We must respond to the call and trust that
His presence is the safest place to be.

Father, we hear Your voice! You're calling us, drawing us
away from the things this world has to offer, and into Your
presence. May we toss aside anything that's holding us
back and run straight to You, Lord. We know You will work
everything for our good, and we're so grateful. Amen!

A PROMISE-KEEPING GOD

Know therefore that the LORD your God is God;
he is the faithful God, keeping his covenant of love
to a thousand generations of those who love him
and keep his commandments.

DEUTERONOMY 7:9 NIV

- -

Parents make promises to their children all the time: "If you get your room cleaned up, we'll go to the mall." "If you stop pestering your sister, I'll give you a special treat." And kids make promises to parents, too: "I'll get along with my sister." "I'll keep my room clean." The reality is, we don't always keep our promises. Our intentions are good. Our follow-through? Not quite so good! Oh, but God always follows through. You can take every single promise in the Bible as truth. He'll do exactly what He said He would do. We have a lot to learn from our promise-keeping God, don't we? What strong families we would be if we always followed through like He does.

Lord, we have so much to learn. We want to be people
of our word. We want to follow through so that others
in our family aren't disappointed. Thank You for teaching
us by example, Father. Amen.

A SONG IN THE NIGHT

*By day the L*ORD* directs his love, at night his song
is with me—a prayer to the God of my life.*
PSALM 42:8 NIV

- - - - - - - - - - - - - - - - - - -

Have you ever had one of those nights when you couldn't
sleep? Maybe you tossed and turned for hours. Here's a
fun way to still your mind and calm your heart: Sing a
worship song. Oh, you don't have to do it aloud (especially
if you share a room) but a silent song of worship will
accomplish several things: quiet your thoughts, put your
focus on God, and remind you that He is in control. God
does so many amazing things for us throughout the day,
but His work doesn't end when the sun goes down. He
wants to croon a lullaby all through the night. So. . .listen!
Perhaps He's singing over you now, encouraging you to
join in. In the stillness, His song rings out, loud and clear.

*Father, what a lovely reminder that Your song is always
with us. Our hearts hear it in the stillness of the night,
whenever everyone around us is silent. Thank You for
placing that song in our hearts, Lord. Amen.*

> *"Watch and pray so that you will not fall into temptation. The spirit is willing, but the flesh is weak."*
> MATTHEW 26:41 NIV

Temptations abound. Open the pantry door and they stare you in the face—cookies, cupcakes, and so on. Walk out the door and they greet you in the face of an angry neighbor or a crazy driver. Head into your workplace or classroom and the temptations don't go away. You're faced with people who try to draw you away from God's best. How do you survive with so many things tugging at you? There's only one way: to watch and pray. If you start your day hyper-focused on the Lord, determined to walk the path He's laid before you, you'll be less likely to buy into the temptations when they come. It's true that our flesh is weak. Oh, but the spirit is willing! And when we're willing to be led and guided by Him, we are sure to overcome!

Lord, we know how weak we are. We've given in to temptation so many times in the past. We're so glad we won't be tempted beyond what we can bear. Please help everyone in the family to stay strong and to run far and fast when temptations come. Amen.

How can a young person stay on the path of purity?
By living according to your word.
PSALM 119:9 NIV

- -

Perhaps you remember a commercial about a particular brand of soap, one advertised to be 99.999 percent pure. What kept it pure? They didn't add "impure" ingredients to it during the "making" process. We're all in the process of being "made" into His image. No matter our age or where we fit in the family, we're all works in progress. Young or old, we've got to guard our hearts so that no impurities are added during the "making." If we keep our purity intact, we'll make an impact for the kingdom of God. Intact = Impact. Now there's a lovely thought.

Lord, we realize that we're all "works in process." You're not done with any of us, thank goodness. While we're "making" we pray that You would guard our hearts, our minds, and our actions so that we can impact the world with the Gospel message. Amen.

*What do workers gain from their toil? I have seen the
burden God has laid on the human race. He has made
everything beautiful in its time.*
ECCLESIASTES 3:9–11 NIV

- -

Have you ever been around a child who was really, really
spoiled? She wanted what she wanted. . .and she wanted
it right now. Maybe you've been that child. And maybe,
even though you're grown up, you still struggle with
wanting what you want. . .and wanting it right now. The
desire to get things quickly doesn't go away as we age.
That's why scriptures like the one above are so important.
They remind us that we don't always get what we want
when we want. Sometimes we have to wait. And wait. And
wait some more. So, no matter what age you are, lay down
your need to get it now and remember that God's timing
is perfect. He's never late. He's always right on time.

*Lord, we confess we don't like to wait. But we're grateful
for the reminder that You make everything perfect in its
time. We can wait on You, Father, knowing that
everything will be beautiful in the end. Amen.*

I have observed something else under the sun. The fastest
runner doesn't always win the race, and the strongest
warrior doesn't always win the battle.
ECCLESIASTES 9:11 NLT

Oh, how we love to run on empty. We do it in our work
life. We do it as students in school. We even do it in our
cars. We go, go, go and then wonder why our tank runs
dry. We crash and burn at the very moment when we
need to be at our best. Our bodies were never made to
go so fast. Sometimes God calls us to a slow, steady race,
not a sprint to the finish line. Where are you today? Are
you running at breakneck speed? Remember, the fastest
winner doesn't always win the race. Sometimes it's really
better to put the brakes on, choose a steady pace, and set
your eye on the goal. You'll still make it, and you might
just make it with a bit of energy left over.

Father, thank You for this reminder that we don't have
to run a hundred miles an hour to meet our goals.
We'll still get there, even at a slower pace. Thank You
for reminding us that our health is an important
part of the equation. Amen.

A STRONG HEART

*Whom have I in heaven but you? And earth has nothing
I desire besides you. My flesh and my heart may fail,
but God is the strength of my heart and my portion forever.*
PSALM 73:25–26 NIV

We have so many desires, so many wishes. We strive after
many things in life. When we're young we want a new
bike, the latest electronic gadget, and so on. When we hit
our late teens we want cool clothes, more electronics, and
perhaps even a car to drive. When we hit our twenties we
want a great job, the perfect home, and the ideal family
environment. It's great to wish for things, but our ultimate
wish, our utmost desire, should be for the Lord. When
we put Him in His proper place, everything else we need
comes into alignment. May we always seek Him above
"stuff." When we get that part right, we will quickly realize
that He never fails us. Stuff comes, and stuff goes, but
the Lord is the strength of our hearts and our portion. . .
forever.

*Lord, sometimes we can't see past all of our wants and
wishes. Thank You for reminding us to keep You in Your
proper place. Our "things" will turn to dust and blow away,
but You, Lord? You'll be with us forever. Praise You! Amen.*

*Pride goes before destruction,
a haughty spirity before a fall.*
PROVERBS 16:18 NIV

There's no room for pride in the family setting. Just about the time someone starts putting themselves up on a pedestal, someone else knocks them down again! The problem with pride is, it points to self at the expense of others. And watch out! One day you might think you're king of the world and the next day you could tumble to the ground, completely humiliated. God knew what He was doing when He warned us to take our eyes off of ourselves and put them squarely on Him. Only when we're God-focused will we avoid destruction.

Father, it's hard to live in a house with so many different people all thinking they're better than others. It's true that pride goes before a fall, and we don't want to watch it happen inside the walls of our own home! Rid us of pride, we pray. May we seek You first, not ourselves. Amen.

STAND FIRM

Therefore, my dear brothers and sisters, stand firm.
Let nothing move you. Always give yourselves fully
to the work of the Lord, because you know that
your labor in the Lord is not in vain.
1 CORINTHIANS 15:58 NIV

- - - - - - - - - - - - - - - - - - - -

Do you remember playing the game "statue" as a kid?
There you stood, trying not to move a muscle, as stiff as
a statue. Until someone made a funny face or tickled you.
Then the statue melted like hot wax! It's hard to be stand
firm, even when you're dedicated to the task. Sometimes
it's just as difficult to stand firm as a believer. You
make up your mind to be faith-filled, then catastrophe
hits. Someone in the family is very ill and has to be
hospitalized. Your strong stance is affected and you waver.
Your knees buckle. But God is good! He never gives up on
us, and we shouldn't give up on ourselves either. Instead,
we do our best to keep on standing, even when it seems
impossible.

We want to keep standing, Father. Keep our knees locked,
Lord! Help us to be fully committed to every task,
so that our labors won't be in vain. Amen!

THE DOOR OF MY LIPS

Set a guard, O Lord, over my mouth;
keep watch over the door of my lips!
PSALM 141:3 ESV

Picture yourself leaving home and locking the door. Then you arrive home, hours later, to find the door cracked open. Fear hits at once. You're afraid to go inside. That door is supposed to be shut, not open for others to enter. We face a similar scenario when we don't keep our lips closed. Oh, we try. We make up our minds not to open our mouths and let gossip slip out, but before long we slip up. We need a lock and key sometimes, don't we! That's what today's scripture is all about. God will set a guard over our mouths and keep watch over the door of our lips if we let Him. Perhaps today would be a great day to ask Him to do just that.

Lord, we'll admit it...sometimes this is one door we leave
cracked open. The door over our lips isn't always shut
tightly. Today we ask You to keep watch over our mouths,
Father. May they only open when You give us
the words to speak. Amen.

*I will praise the L*ORD*, who counsels me;*
even at night my heart instructs me.
PSALM 16:7 NIV

- -

Sometimes we have to get to a really quiet place to hear
the voice of the Lord more clearly. He often speaks most
clearly to us in the wee hours of the night when we're in a
near-sleep state. Without the craziness of the day (horns
honking, kids bickering, dishes clinking, TV blaring, co-
workers chattering) we are better able to hear His voice.
Some of the best counsel we will ever receive comes in
still, quiet moments such as this. The next time you're
seeking direction, tuck yourself in bed, turn off the light,
and wait until you're nearly asleep. Perhaps, in that cozy
spot, your heavenly Father will whisper guiding words
into your ear.

Father, we love those still, quiet moments when we're
nearly asleep. Thank You for giving us direction when
we're best able to hear, Lord. What a blissful time
with You. We're so grateful. Amen.

A MEMBER OF THE FAMILY

Consequently, you are no longer foreigners
and strangers, but fellow citizens with God's people
and also members of his household.
EPHESIANS 2:19 NIV

Isn't it wonderful to be the member of a family? People in families have a sense of belonging. They know there's someone out there who has their back. That's just how it is in God's family. When we link arms with other believers, when we stand together, we're part of something larger than ourselves. We aren't strangers, aliens. We're fellow citizens, members of the same household. . .God's household. Isn't it wonderful to be included, to have like-minded people gathered around us, no matter what we're going through? Families are a part of the Lord's glorious plan for our lives, and we're grateful for them.

Father, You are, indeed, our Father. We are Your children,
part of Your royal family. To be a member of that family
is such an honor, Lord. Thank You for surrounding us with
people who truly care about us. We love You, Father. Amen.

Genesis
1:27 40
9:13 18
50:20 114

Exodus
40:34 168

Deuteronomy
7:9 176

Joshua
1: 7–9 135
1:8 152
24:15 .90

Ruth
1:16 86
3:9 119

1 Samuel
17:4 16
18:1–3 .44

2 Chronicles
7:14 9

Job
38:41 45

Psalm
3:3 150
3:5 58
5:11 97
9:2 73
16:7 186
16:8 61
16:9 98
23:2 171
30:11 26
31:9 51
31:24 131
34:17 .123
37:5 117
42:8 177
61:2 146
62:1–2 87
73:25–26 182
84:11 164
90:14 147
90:17 59
91:5 172
95:6 110

101:2–3 72
119:9 179
119:105 5
132:15 46
133:1 112
139:13–14 163
141:3 185
144:15 133
145:4 24

Proverbs
3:5–6 165
3:12 54
3:24 63
4:23 162
8:32–33 138
11:29 89
12:25 159
14:23 94
15:20 96
16:18 183
17:9 167
17:22 141
19:11 153
20:7 77
20:11 157

22:6 22
24:5 29
25:21 13
29:18 47

Ecclesiastes
3:1 144
3:9–11 180
3:11 91
9:11 181
12:1 155

Isaiah
1:18 169
40:29–30 149

Jeremiah
1:4–5 160
29:11 55

Jonah
1:3 .14

Matthew
5:14 41
5:16 . . . . 50, 125

6:27	122
6:34	120
7:11	74
10:31	15
12:33	57
18:12	93
24:14	108
26:41	178

Mark

11:23	154
12:30–31	11

Luke

1:13	48
4:42	82
6:22	76
6:38	20, 71
10:30	99
13:24	34
22:14–16	121

John

14:15	128
15:13	35

15:16	145
15:18	27
16:33	56

Acts

4:12	105
16:25	84
20:35	52

Romans

3:23–24	43
7:19–20	25
8:1	20
8:5	106
8:28	161, 175
8:38–39	100
11:29	33
12:2	60
15:4	78
15:7	8

1 Corinthians

12:14	42
14:33	104
15:58	184

2 Corinthians

2:14	66
5:17	37
6:3	129

Galatians

1:10	7, 130
5:1	143

Ephesians

2:19	187
3:14-15	70
3:20-21	166
4:2	38
4:2-3	19
4:26	69
4:29	80
4:31-32	23
5:15-17	113
6:10-11	17

Philippians

2:14-16	10
2:3	62
3:13-14	68

3:14	39
4:13	75
4:6	103
4:19	67

Colossians

1:11	49
1:13-14	174
1:17	126
3:8	101
3:12	31
3:23	109

1 Thessalonians

5:12	83

2 Thessalonians

3:11	142

1 Timothy

4:12	136
5:1-2	173
6:6	151
6:6-8	36
6:10	95

2 Timothy

1:6....................115
1:7....................170
2:15....................30
3:15....................12

Titus

3:2....................137

Philemon

1:4....................88

Hebrews

10:25 148
11:30....................79
12:1-2....................127
13:5....................158

James

1:2-3....................81
1:12....................124
1:19-20 118
2:1....................107
2:15-17....................140
3:14....................139
5:13....................53, 92

1 Peter

2:5....................156
3:3-4 134
3:9....................65

1 John

1:5-6....................28
1:9....................85
2:15....................116
3:1....................132
3:18....................64
5:14-15....................32

3 John

1:11....................102

Revelation

2:17 111